I Would Have Said Yes A Family's Journey With Autism—
wow, the title alone makes every parent pause and examine
his or her heart. It entices the reader. Lisa's testimony is not
only emotional but also inspiring and courageous! Thank
you, Lisa, Ron, Justin, Daniel, and Allie for sharing your
journey with others!

Margaret Carodine-Whitaker
Head of School
St. Timothy Christian Academy

Amid a tumultuous week of uncertainty about our son's
future, up popped an encouraging message from author
Lisa Simmons. "Always follow your instinct . . . even
when all around you disagree." This truly felt like a voice
straight from heaven telling me not to give up on myself
or my son. Thank you, Lisa. Your journey and your words
made a difference in my life.

Jane Jarrell
Author and account executive,
Tricom Communications

With candor, vulnerability, and openness, Lisa Simmons
draws you into her world of parenting a special needs
child. Her viewpoint of life encourages and challenges
you—in whatever situation you face—to not become a
victim, but to be a victor! I Would Have Said, "Yes," is a
must-read for all who seek to know more of God.

Edwina Patterson

T0165004

Lisa Simmons shares the deepest sorrows, joys, and frustrations of a mother's heart. Her honesty and transparency are so refreshing. This book is filled with insights and wise application of biblical principles. Her faith and perseverance is inspiring and I have been blessed by her story.

Susie Hawkins
Author—From One Ministry Wife to Another

I WOULD HAVE SAID YES

A Family's Journey with Autism

LISA SIMMONS

WESTBOW
PRESS
A DIVISION OF THOMAS NELSON

WestBow Press books may be ordered through booksellers or by contacting:

WestBow Press
A Division of Thomas Nelson
1663 Liberty Drive
Bloomington, IN 47403
www.westbowpress.com
1-(866) 928-1240

Because of the dynamic nature of the Internet, any web addresses or
links contained in this book may have changed since publication and
may no longer be valid. The views expressed in this work are solely those
of the author and do not necessarily reflect the views of the publisher,
and the publisher hereby disclaims any responsibility for them.

Any people depicted in stock imagery provided by Thinkstock are
models, and such images are being used for illustrative purposes only.

Certain stock imagery © Thinkstock.

ISBN: 978-1-4497-4874-6 (e)
ISBN: 978-1-4497-4873-9 (sc)

Library of Congress Control Number: 2012906944

Printed in the United States of America

WestBow Press rev. date: 06/25/2012

ACKNOWLEDGEMENTS

I would like to first thank God for the privilege of sharing our family's story in a way that hopefully demonstrates His sovereignty and mercy. While people can influence our decisions, attitudes and behaviors, ultimately our greatest influence must come from the one who created our "inmost being" if we are to have peace. Our lives are a tapestry of God moments and I'm so thankful to be a tiny thread in His masterpiece.

To my husband Ron, who tirelessly listened to my complaining, whining, and frustration in writing this book. It was far more difficult to write than I had anticipated, but you hung in there with me. You remembered more than I thought you possibly could about Daniel's challenges, since you were busy building a career and supporting our family. Daniel's success comes from your commitment to a "whatever it takes" attitude. Grateful does not begin to cover what's in my heart.

To Justin and Allie Beth, thank you. I know you didn't realize anything was different about Daniel for much of your childhoods. I'm so thankful however, that once you did understand the difference in your sibling relationships versus other families, you did not waver in your love for your brother. Did you get frustrated at times? Were there moments when you said, "If only . . . ."? Yes, I'm sure. But I know how you both feel about Daniel and realize the blessings you have because of him. Daniel has a great treasure in having a brother and sister like you two.

To my mother-in-law Dorothy, there are no words. You were there so many times when I just needed a break. What would I have done without your support and love through our many trials and triumphs. You are a huge blessing to our entire family, but especially to me.

Daniel, how could we have said otherwise?

CONTENTS

FOREWORD

A great many people now look at autism from a "whole body" perspective, not just from a behavioral or biomedical point of view. Many professionals have looked at autism as a "whole family" condition. Autism's impact on the family—on moms, dads, siblings, grandparents, aunts, and uncles—is tangible and can be devastating. Those of us who provide programs and services, including education, need to be diligent in helping the family as well as the child find ways to be healthy and work together to ensure success for everyone. The happier the family, the happier the child will become. As most of us realize, however, this is easier said than done. And that is precisely why we must make a concerted effort to address family needs while we are helping the child.

Moms and dads are heartfelt in their desire to help their child, but they approach the situation from very different angles—and these often can be at odds with each other. Parents may not recognize or accept that different gender roles and perceptions can affect the way each person relates to the diagnosis itself, to understanding autism and making decisions about treatment. Often, the result is that parents feel alienated from one another, and the child's education is delegated to Mom, who—willingly or not—becomes responsible for learning about autism, unearthing possible sources of assistance, and deciding on treatment. Dad, on the other hand, assumes the responsibility for providing financially for the family, often staying an arm's length away from becoming more involved in care and treatment.

Couples can easily drift apart at this delicate juncture. Dad goes off to work each morning, and Mom starts to resent his "freedom." He doesn't have to deal with the child's relentless meltdowns. He doesn't have to clean up yet another mess the child created or deal with strangers' stares or whispers when the child reacts because the grocery store is out of the child's favorite cereal. For Mom, autism requires her attention 24/7 and becomes a never never-ending (and often thankless) job. She often feels alone and unappreciated. In turn, Dad feels alienated. Without regular, direct exposure to the child, he doesn't learn how to handle autism, and feels inadequate when he tries. He resents that his wife devotes all her time to the child and that she no longer has time for him. As Mom reaches out to others for information and support more and more, Dad no longer feels needed, except for his paycheck. Mom can inadvertently shut Dad out of the information loop, setting up a pattern of learned helplessness—the inability to do something because of a lack of exposure to or experience in doing it.

I Would Have Said Yes is one mother's spiritual ride through her own life journey and that of her son Daniel, who has an autism spectrum disorder (ASD). Lisa Simmons describes the ups and downs of her struggles and triumphs related to a condition that was unfamiliar to her until Daniel was diagnosed. She weaves the perspectives of many people, including her husband and neurotypical children, in a way that allows readers to feel what she was feeling at the impactful moments. Her belief in God and her enduring faith gave her the strength during the trying times and allowed her to see the joy in quirky things Daniel did. Ultimately, she realized that she'd known all along that the experience would be priceless, based on seeing all that Daniel brought—and continues to bring—to his family and the world around him. I would wholeheartedly recommend this book to every family who has a child on the spectrum.

If you view autism as a "dis-ability," it will "dis-able" your family and your lives. See it, rather, as a *different* ability, recognizing that it affects the entire family (even the dog). Learn to notice the positive aspects of autism. They are there; you just need to see them. When things get out of control and you lose your direction, seek outside help. Support groups, a good friend, trained counselors, or a spiritual connection are all ways to navigate the often choppy seas of life in general, but they can be life preservers for families of children with ASD. Find ways that help you stay afloat—as an individual, as a couple, and as a family—when dark skies loom overhead. Always keep your focus on the child and his needs, but do not neglect yourself or other members of your family. You are all equally important. To truly help your child, you often need to first find ways to help yourself accept and love him, autism included. Your family is only as strong as its weakest link. Lisa Simmons walks you through this journey in her own way.

James Ball, EdD, BCBA-D

President and Chief Executive Officer
JB Autism Consulting

Executive Chair
National Board of Directors
The Autism Society

Board Member
Autism Consultant
The Healing Hands of Christ Foundation

Author of the award-winning book *Early Intervention and Autism: Real-Life Questions; Real-Life Answers*

INTRODUCTION

Not only this, but we also rejoice in sufferings, knowing that suffering produces endurance, and endurance, character, and character, hope. And hope does not disappoint, because the love of God has been poured out in our hearts through the Holy Spirit who was given to us (ROMANS 5:3-5).

What would happen in our lives if God asked our permission before he gave us any new blessing or hardship? What would our answer be? Well, I'd say yes to the blessings and no to the hardships. Who in his right mind would say, "Yes, Lord, I'm ready for a painful circumstance in my life right about now, so go ahead—hit me with your best shot." Certainly, no one would ask willingly for a traumatic or difficult condition or circumstance in the life of his or her child. But I've heard story after story from people who say, "The lessons I learned by going through this circumstance were worth the pain of whatever I dealt with." Even that is a tough thing to say, in my opinion.

Shortly after moving to Dallas, Texas, in 1985 with my husband, my three-year-old son, Justin, and newborn son, Daniel, we joined a church in downtown Dallas. We wanted to get involved as soon as possible with other young married couples who shared our values and interests. We found a great group of couples our age.

Some did not have children and some were just beginning to start their families, but they all made us feel that we had found our new home.

On one occasion in our class on Sunday morning, we had a guest speaker named Marion. She told about her family—her husband, three daughters, and a son. The part of her story that I found so memorable is what led to the title of this book. One of her daughters, six years old at the time, was on her way to church camp with another family. They were in a terrible car accident, and her little girl was killed. I can't imagine the horror and agony of losing a child, but I could feel her heartbreak as she told the story. She continued sharing that her husband had spoken at the funeral of their precious daughter. While trying his best to maintain composure, he had described a make-believe scenario. He had said, "If God had told me six years ago that he had a little girl for me"—he had gone on to describe his daughter—"but if I wanted her, I could only have her for six years, through a broken heart and many tears, I would have said yes."

That was twenty-six years ago, and those words have stuck with me all these years. I have never lost a child through death, but I have wondered if I would be strong enough to say yes if God asked me to carry a burden so difficult. Fortunately, God does not ask. I'm afraid if he did, we would all say no to the hardships and miss some incredible growth and blessings. Sometimes, the sad, tragic, difficult, and painful parts of life are what give the seemingly boring, mundane, and drab parts of life . . . well . . . *life*.

I pray that this book inspires you to not give up when life hits you so hard that you think you won't be able to take the next breath. But more than that, I hope you will see that God is in all things and can create the most beautiful blessings from your circumstances, if you let Him.

I WOULD HAVE SAID YES

What if God asked our permission
To give us each child whom he had commissioned
To be our child to have and hold
To teach His ways as they grow old?

Knowing your child
As you know him or her
Would you have said yes
If God had conferred?

"The child I give
Is a little boy
Who looks like you.
Is he your choice?

"When he screams in the car
Will you still be glad
Though nothing quiets
This boy you've had?

"When 'they' look in your eyes
Saying, 'He can't achieve'
Will you still say yes?
Will you still believe?

"Then there'll be times
With your heart full of love
You'll find that his journey
Is way too tough.

"You'll try and you'll cry
'God, please just fix it'
But I'll say that my grace
Must be sufficient.

"His smile will bring joy
His demeanor a pleasure
This boy that you'll raise
Is my greatest treasure.

"So I'll ask you once more
Will you have what it takes
To never give up
Even when your heart breaks?

"For all the trials and turmoil
That he'll have to go through
Just to reach manhood
Will that bother you?

"Will you teach him My ways
And be there for him?
Will you show him My love
When your patience wears thin?

"Will you do all of this
An indefinite time
Knowing all along
That he's always been mine?"

I would have said yes.

CHAPTER 1

What If God Asked?

I pray that the God of our Lord Jesus Christ, the Father of glory, may give you spiritual wisdom and revelation in your growing knowledge of him, since the eyes of your heart have been enlightened so that you may know what is the hope of his calling (Ephesians 1:17).

I was like most girls. I dreamed of growing up, going to college, becoming a teacher, getting married, having children—*"Ta-da! I'm done!"* That was the life I'd envisioned. It pretty much happened that way, although the order got a little scrambled. I did grow up, and I did go to college, but I married while I was still in college and had my first baby, Justin, just before starting my student teaching. Whew! Quite a whirlwind of activity for a three-and-a-half-year period, but I did it. I graduated and became a teacher—what I'd always wanted to be.

My husband, Ron, continued working full-time while going to school part-time. Because of his part-time status as a student, it took him ten years to complete his undergraduate degree. He likes to joke that he crammed four years into ten. Obviously, he crammed a lot more into those ten years than just a college education.

One of the professors at Southern Arkansas University suggested that I should quit school or work and go to school part-time, so that Ron could finish his degree first. I understand why that seemed logical to her. She obviously saw that Ron was incredibly gifted and could make great strides in the business world. She didn't factor in, however, my determination to get a degree. No one in my family had ever been to college. Some of them had barely graduated high school. I had to finish. I would later use that same determination for something much more important than a college degree.

Our lives were stressful. Before we married, Ron got a full-time job in the mailroom at Murphy Oil Corporation. He started in August, a month before his nineteenth birthday. We'd been engaged for two months and were planning a June wedding. Now that he had a great (in our minds) job with benefits, we moved the wedding date to March, over spring break. We'd have time for a short honeymoon before returning to school and work.

We would have moved the wedding up even sooner, but I wasn't willing to get married as a teenager. I'd seen too many friends and family members get married in their teens, only to struggle, having no money, no education, and no prospects for a better life. I promised myself I would never do that. My twentieth birthday was February 12, 1980. We got married in March. Goal achieved!

Nine months after we were married, I found out I was pregnant. I was beginning the first semester of my senior year and planned to graduate in May 1982. Once I knew that the baby was due in September 1981, I "put the pedal to the metal" and signed up for as many classes as possible. By taking nineteen hours on campus and one correspondence course, I would have only my student teaching to complete after the baby was born. That meant I could finish school by December 1981, instead of May 1982.

I knew it would be challenging. I was driving an eighty-mile round trip—from El Dorado, where we lived, to the main campus of SAU in Magnolia—five days a week. Thank goodness gasoline prices were not what they are now. With a 9:00 a.m. class and suffering from morning sickness, there were many days when I wanted to give up. Thinking about *not* achieving my goal of becoming a teacher kept me going. I couldn't let that happen. I decided that if I was failing any course by the last opportunity to drop a class, I would drop that class, but I wouldn't quit. By the time the final drop-date came, I had a B average, so I plunged ahead.

In addition to being eight months pregnant, I suffered through a summer of record-breaking heat. I knew I had to finish that correspondence course before the baby came. He was due August 25, but I couldn't seem to get motivated. It must have been around August 26 when I decided, *If I'm going to be pregnant for the rest of my life,*

I might as well do something productive. On September 9, I finished the correspondence course, put it in the mailbox, and sat down on the couch. I felt a twinge of pain in my back. I was in labor. Justin Ronald Simmons was born the next day, September 10, 1981.

When Justin was five weeks old, I began my student teaching. I'd thought taking nineteen hours in one semester was difficult, but having a five-week-old baby and no sleep while working with twenty-nine second graders all day was next to impossible. That entire time was a blur. If I could just hang on until Christmas, I'd told myself, it would all be over. I would have my degree and could stay home with Justin until the following fall, when I would start my first teaching job.

You may be noticing a pattern: what I plan rarely seems to happen—at least not the way I expect it to happen. During the Christmas holidays, I got a phone call from the El Dorado Independent School District office. The teacher under whom I'd student taught was leaving and wouldn't be returning after Christmas. Since I'd been in her class half of the fall semester, they thought I was the perfect person to take over her position in January.

I wanted to cry. I probably did cry. If Ron hadn't overheard the conversation, I might not have told him about it. But Ron was salivating at the idea of additional income, and I can't blame him. He'd been carrying the financial weight of a family plus my school expenses for eighteen months. I just wanted to sleep. I took the job instead.

Even though I'd finally achieved my goal of being a teacher, I wanted more than anything to stay home with my new baby. But since I'd worked so hard for that degree, I felt like I'd be letting everyone—including myself—down if I didn't at least give this opportunity a chance. So that's what I did for about eighteen months.

I came home to be a full-time mom at the end of the 1982-83 school year. It wasn't a tough decision, but it was a tough transition. My quitting work essentially cut our household income in half. We were earning below the poverty line while trying to maintain an above-median-income living. There wasn't a lot of fun going on in our house, to say the least. I had a toddler, a house, a car, and a husband, but no time, no money, and no energy to enjoy life. This wasn't part of the dream.

For some reason, in the midst of our chaotic lives, I began to pray about having another baby. According to anyone's perspective but mine, this wasn't a good idea, considering our circumstances. Ron was perfectly happy with one child. He'd said more than once that he wouldn't be upset or unhappy if we didn't have any more children. "Why mess with perfection?" he'd joke. But I just couldn't get the idea of having at least two children (and possibly more) out of my head.

After I'd prayed for a while and enlisted some of my friends to pray as well, Ron turned to me one night as we were driving down Northwest Avenue and said, "I think we should try to have another baby." This was totally out of the blue, and it was so far from what he had said in the past that I could hardly believe he was saying it. Then I remembered my prayer. *Okay, God. This must be*

Your idea. By April 1984, I was pregnant with our second child. Little did we realize the crazy adventure we would experience in the following months.

In October 1984, Ron began sending out résumés to different companies in Dallas. He'd told me from the beginning of our marriage that we probably wouldn't live in El Dorado forever. I didn't really give that much thought; honestly, I couldn't conceive of living somewhere else. But when a friend of his who worked at Murphy moved back to her hometown of Dallas, he told her to keep her eye out for job opportunities for him.

I still didn't get it, even when he started receiving the *Dallas Morning News.* When he asked me to help him by typing the résumé, I felt like he'd asked me to type my own obituary. I'd never lived anywhere else and had no desire to do so. I didn't want to pray about it. I didn't even want to talk about it.

In the back of my mind, I was saying, *There's no way he's going to get another job. He's got the best job a guy could have who doesn't have his degree yet.* He'd moved from the mailroom to the accounting department to the benefits department—all within two years. For someone without a degree, he was doing all right.

I should have realized when he refused to stay in the mailroom that this was a man on a mission. However, when he'd say, "I applied for the position of accountant," or "I interviewed for a position as benefit analyst," I'd just look at him. I thought he had about as much chance of winning the presidential nomination as he did of moving up at Murphy Oil Corporation without a degree or without the last name Murphy.

I was a "Negative Nellie," but each time—without fail—he got the position for which he applied. Of course, the biggest argument for not wanting him to apply for a job in Texas—or any other state, for that matter—was "All of my family lives in El Dorado, and we're about to have another baby, and . . . and . . . and . . ." I had all of my reasons for staying ready, just in case he did get a job offer.

Shortly after sending Ron's résumé to various companies, he got a call from Parkland Hospital in Dallas. They wanted him to interview for a job in their human resources department. *Breathe. Breathe*, I kept telling myself. *It's just an interview.* We drove to Dallas in our little blue Ford Escort with our three-year-old son, Justin. I felt like we may as well have been driving to New York City. It was so overwhelming.

We checked into our hotel. *Okay, this part is fun*, I thought. *I'll just pretend we're on a mini vacation.* The interview went well, and we actually enjoyed our time in Dallas. Just driving around, looking at the tall buildings and craziness of the traffic, was kind of exciting. Not exciting enough for me to want to move there, but exciting for a visit. We even looked at different neighborhoods. I was amazed at the cost of houses and wondered how anyone could ever make enough money to afford to live there. Our little three-bedroom, one-bath home in El Dorado had cost less than $35,000. A similar home in a suburb of Dallas was more than twice as much.

We drove back to El Dorado with so many thoughts swirling in our heads. I believe Ron was really excited about the possibility of moving. He wanted to stretch his mind and explore what other opportunities lay ahead. He had moved around a lot as a child. He'd lived in a different city and had gone to a different school about every two years or so until he reached eighth grade. At this point, however, he had lived in one place for more than ten years. It was time to move on. I, on the other hand, was beyond scared. I just couldn't fathom a life outside of family, friends, and familiarity. I grew up in El Dorado, went to school in El Dorado, and planned to die in El Dorado! Within a few days, we got the call that I hoped would come: "We're sorry; you didn't get the job." I know it sounds terrible, but I was so relieved. I was a very insecure and quite selfish young wife and mom. When I saw how disappointed Ron was, I felt terrible—not so much that I changed my mind about moving, but I did feel sorry for him.

We went on living as usual. We began decorating the nursery and choosing names for the new baby. Even though we didn't know the sex, we decided on Daniel if it was a boy. Around the same time, Ron received a book of his father's family ancestry. He read that one of his distant relatives was William Barrett Travis of Alamo fame, so we decided that if we had another boy, his name would be Daniel Travis.

Now that the name of the baby was settled, there was nothing to do except wait for Christmas and then for the baby to arrive toward the end of January. Once again, however, my calm "leave-my-life-as-is" plans were thwarted. We got a phone call just before Christmas from a bank in Dallas. They had gotten Ron's name from someone at Parkland Hospital. *What? How did that happen?* I wondered. North Dallas Bank wanted him to come for an interview on December 27. Honestly, I really wasn't that worried about this interview. I figured it would go in similar fashion to the other interview. They would be impressed with him, but since he didn't have his degree, they would have to choose someone else. But that is not what happened. Just after New Year's, we got a call from North Dallas Bank, asking Ron if he would accept the position. *What?* I screamed in my head. *No way! How can we take a new job so far away from home, when I'm just weeks—more like days—away from delivering a baby?*

When Ron told his boss at Murphy about the job offer, he immediately offered Ron a raise to stay. I should have been excited about the raise, but it really made me mad. A raise? Now? Why didn't he deserve a raise yesterday or last week? Ron went back to the bank and told them what his boss had offered. They immediately offered more. The negotiations went back and forth for most of the afternoon. I was lying on the bed, praying each time Ron would call. I'm not one to look for signs from God, but I really needed confirmation on this decision. I told Ron I was going to tell God that if his current boss offered X amount, we would stay in El Dorado. Ron called back just a few minutes later. His boss had offered five hundred dollars less than what we had decided was our "stay" number. Five hundred dollars! I almost said, "Okay, God, five hundred dollars is not that big of a difference. Are you sure?" But I didn't. We both said, "We're moving." I was totally at peace. I was shocked at how peaceful the decision was, when only moments before I'd been squirming over it. We accepted the offer from North Dallas Bank. Ron would start work February 4, 1985.

Daniel Travis Simmons was born just after midnight, January 24, 1985-only eleven days before Ron was to start his new job in Dallas. No worries. Even though we had sold our house to my cousin and his family, they were nice enough to allow me to stay there until at least the six-week well-check appointment with my doctor and our pediatrician. In my mind, I thought I could coast for a while longer. I was wrong.

That year we had an unusual winter snowstorm just before Ron left our home in El Dorado for Dallas on Sunday, February 3. He was to start his job on Monday, February 4. We decided that he would attempt the drive to Dallas anyway. Thankfully, the roads cleared just about an hour and a half from town. As soon as Ron drove away, I felt so empty and lonely. Because the least bit of ice or snow on El Dorado roads would shut down the entire city down for days. I was snowed in—no one could come to see me and I couldn't go anywhere. Fortunately, my daddy was not afraid to drive in the snow, especially when I called, crying, "Can I come to your house?"

Of course, Daddy came to pick up me and the kids. So there we were: Justin, Daniel, and I, sitting on my parents' couch, wondering what in the world was happening. I truly felt like I was in another realm. My middle sister, Lynda, with her new baby, Haley, who was only four months old, as well as my youngest sister, Lori, who was sixteen was there. Then the phone rang. There's nothing unusual about the phone ringing in the middle of the day, especially with a sixteen-year-old in the house, but this phone call was not a boyfriend or someone just calling to chat. It was my aunt, who had been taking care of my elderly grandmother. My grandmother, who had lived two houses down from me all of my life, had just passed away from congestive heart failure.

There were no cell phones, so I had to wait until Ron called after he reached Dallas to tell him about my grandmother's death. He was torn as to what to do. Should he turn around and come home, and tell the bank that he couldn't begin work on Monday after all? Or should he stay, start his job, and then come home? There just was no easy answer. We decided that he should stay in Dallas.

That week felt like the longest week of my life. After leaving my parent's house that day, not only was I alone with two babies, but we also were mourning the loss of someone who had been such a huge part of our lives. My mom, the youngest child in her family, was particularly close to her mother. Maw Maw, as we called my grandmother, was a stable part of my childhood, so it was difficult to imagine not going over to her house just to talk to her or seeing her walking over to have supper with us. Who would help me with my sewing projects? Would Justin even remember her? He was only three. After the funeral, I called Ron and cried, "Come get me." I knew that I needed to be with my husband and feel the significance of my own little family. By the time he came home that Friday evening, we were ready to pack up and leave Arkansas after only one week of his being away, instead of six.

I had started packing while I was pregnant, so it didn't take very long for us to finish putting our entire small household in a U-Haul and head west. I think I was in such a daze from all that had taken place over the last few weeks that I didn't really consider what my mom must have been feeling. I remember her saying to Daniel as she held him one last time before we left, "Justin will have to tell you all about me, because I won't be there with you like I was with him." I'd said, "Mom, we're moving to Dallas, not China. We'll be back, and you can come there." That was very bold of me, considering I'd been a basket case about this move just a few weeks before. Little did I know how prophetic her words would be.

I turned twenty-five just two days after we moved into our rented house in North Dallas. I remember being so excited that there were multiple restaurants from which to choose to celebrate my birthday, unlike our small hometown of El Dorado, where the selection was limited. I had seen the wonderful commercials about a chain seafood restaurant and thought it would be so great to go to such a fancy restaurant. So that's where we went for my twenty-fifth birthday. I thought, *It doesn't get better than this.*

I did not hate living in Dallas as much as I thought I would. Of course, I kept my doors locked at home and in the car, and I would not drive anywhere by myself. As soon as Ron got home from work, we would have dinner and then go for a drive. On the weekends, we would try to find something fun to do, like visiting the Dallas Zoo, or going to a movie, or just walking the mall. We did go home to El Dorado about two weeks after moving. I was ready for a visit with my family, and I didn't want my mother's prediction to come true. It was different going home as a visitor, but it was good to see everyone, even after being gone such a brief time.

We had been in Dallas exactly one month when a couple who were friends of ours from El Dorado came to visit for the weekend. It was so nice to see familiar faces. They had a three-year-old boy, and Justin enjoyed having a playmate his own age. No sooner had our friends left than we got a phone call from my dad, saying that my mom had been flown by helicopter to Schumpert Hospital in Shreveport. She had been admitted into the hospital in El Dorado with a migraine a week earlier, just after our visit home. She'd stayed in the hospital over the weekend, and upon her release, her doctor prescribed Valium and told her the headache was related to stress. At the time, the diagnosis made sense. After all, she had just lost her mother. Her oldest daughter and two grandchildren had moved out of the state. She was working full-time, and she was helping one daughter with a newborn and had another daughter who was sixteen. That's enough to cause anyone a migraine. This was not, however, just a headache or even a migraine. This was an aneurysm.

It had been slowly leaking for about three weeks, causing the headaches. It finally burst and caused a massive stroke. The doctors didn't have much hope, but since she was only forty-three years old, they wanted to try everything possible. When my dad said they didn't think she was going to make it, I felt my knees buckle. Ron was there to catch me, but I just kept saying, "No, no, no! This can't be happening."

We quickly packed, but I wouldn't let myself put a dress in the suitcase. I felt like packing a dress meant there was going to be a funeral. There couldn't be a funeral again. Hadn't we had a funeral barely six weeks ago? By the time we reached the hospital, all of my family was there to meet us. One of my uncles said that my mother had made a slight improvement. They wanted me to go in to see her, but I resisted for as long as I could—I didn't want to see my mother, one of the strongest women I knew, in such a weak and sad condition. After more encouragement from my relatives, I did go in to her ICU cubicle. It was worse than I'd thought. I could barely look at her, with all the wires and tubes everywhere. This was not my mother; at least, not the one I had left just a few weeks ago. I went back to the waiting room more numb than when I had entered a few hours earlier. I know people were talking to me, but I just sat there, holding my six-week-old baby and staring into space. Three days later, the life support was removed after all the tests for brain activity were negative. My mother died on March 12. We had her funeral three days later, on Ron's and my fifth wedding anniversary.

Enough! I wanted to scream at this point. Obviously, I was in a depressed state. Having a baby, moving from my home, and losing my grandmother and mother, all in a two-month period, had taken a toll on my body, heart, and mind. I cried every day. Sometimes I sobbed uncontrollably while Justin stood beside my chair, staring at me. My children were the only things that kept me sane. I went to the doctor, because I couldn't seem to breathe. I could breathe in and out, but I couldn't get a good deep breath. I felt like I was drowning or like someone was standing on my oxygen hose. I began to think that there was something seriously wrong with me. My doctor gave me a prescription for Valium, because

I was having stress-related panic attacks. I decided that I had to get a grip. I did not want to be drugged while trying to care for my family. That, in my mind, was not only irresponsible but impossible.

Since our faith is very important to us, we found a church to attend within a couple of months of moving. Really, *it* found us. One Sunday morning, the doorbell rang. I was home with the boys while Ron was out of town. I cautiously opened the door to find two rather elderly ladies standing on the front porch. They introduced themselves and explained that they were visiting people who might not attend church anywhere. The church they represented was a large downtown church in Dallas. They went on to tell me how they attended the eight o'clock service and then the nine o'clock Bible Fellowship hour and spent the eleven o'clock hour inviting people to church. (I still think this is a brilliant idea). I filled out the information packet they handed me and gave it back. They left and I didn't really give it much more thought. The next day I received a call from someone from that church asking if they could come for a visit that evening. At around seven o'clock that night there were three people sitting on my couch from the young married department of the church-Wade and Melissa Allen and Karol Ladd.

God had brought this group of people to us at exactly the right time.

Even though it was a very large downtown church, we soon found a group of friends with which to enjoy this stage of life. Wade and Melissa as well as Karol and her husband Curt became close friends. Curt owned an insurance business and was looking for a part-time secretary. Even though the last thing I'd wanted to do was work outside the home again, I decided to give it a try. I began working for Curt and another insurance agent, Mike Reppert. twenty hours a week. It forced me out of the dark hole in which I'd hidden myself during the last six months. It created the need to learn to drive in Dallas and challenged me to interact with people I never would have otherwise, It worked better than Valium would have.

CHAPTER 2

He Screams in the Car

I have no ease; I have no quietness; I cannot rest; turmoil has come upon me (JOB 3:26).

From the moment they lay Daniel in my arms, I sensed something was wrong. I tried to allay my fears by telling myself it was nonsense. We had a normal delivery with the exception of the doctor being delayed about fifteen minutes, causing me to have to subdue my desire to push for what seemed more like eternity, so I had no logical reason to feel that way. The doctor had given us a slight scare the week before Daniel was born, when he said in a concerned tone, "You're holding a lot of water." When I asked if that was a bad thing, he said, "Well, it could mean that there's something wrong with the baby, like spina bifida or cerebral palsy." I remember lying on the table in the doctor's office as he told me this bit of news—less than one week before delivery—thinking,

What is he saying? How could he tell me this now? When I told Ron about the bombshell that had been dropped on me, he was so mad that he threatened to call the doctor and tell him what he thought of him. But I didn't want the doctor angry with me at the time of delivery, so I convinced Ron to let it go. Perhaps the doctor's words were still rambling around in my head, and that's why I felt a sense of unease.

Even with the death of my grandmother and mother, the quick move, and adjusting to a new environment, I continued to have those lingering thoughts that something was wrong with Daniel. He had a constantly furrowed brow. It was like he was saying, "What just happened, and how do I get back to where I was?" I never said anything to anyone about my feelings, not even to Ron.

I minored in psychology in college. My intention was to teach school for a while and then eventually become a counselor. I love helping people; I enjoy listening to their problems and helping them find solutions. I think that's what drew me to teaching in the first place. Teachers are the first people we encounter, besides our parents, who help us with our problems. Through my study of psychology, I had learned the philosophies of Sigmund Freud. In particular, Freud's theory on the effects of the mother's attitudes and behaviors on her children began to run through my head. So when Daniel didn't smile much, or when he had an unusual fear response when left lying on his back, or when he screamed every time we started driving in a car, I assumed it was my fault. I had been so consumed with sadness during his first six months of life that he rarely saw me smile. He probably felt my fear of being in an unfamiliar city with an unfamiliar lifestyle. He probably sensed my uneasiness with driving in Dallas traffic. Yes, it was surely my fault.

I began to force myself to smile. I literally had to smile consciously in front of Daniel. The funny thing about smiling and laughing is that it really can have a positive effect on your demeanor. Even when things around you haven't changed, smiling, even if it's forced, can change your attitude. I also found ways to keep Daniel from having his unusual fear response. When I placed him on his back to put his clothes on or change his diaper, I had to keep my hand (or a blanket or a stuffed animal) on his tummy. If he were left for even a few seconds with no pressure on his body, he would panic—his arms would fling out as if he was falling. This reaction is normal in all babies, as their fear of falling is instinctual, but it was the way Daniel's body would stiffen that worried me, particularly because it was followed by a blood-curdling scream. He not only had this response when left on his back but when he was in his swing as well. As soon as the swing went back and forth a couple of times, his arms would stiffen, he'd hold his breath, he'd turn red, and then he'd *scream*! We had to get rid of the baby swing and tell the church nursery workers not to put him in one.

I talked to his Daniel's pediatrician about these unusual behaviors, but the doctor didn't find anything alarming about them. He said whatever I was doing was working, so I should keep doing that. He also wasn't too concerned that Daniel was on the low side of the achievement scale. Now, I'm not a mom who thinks her children have to be the biggest, best, and brightest, and I consciously avoided comparing Daniel's abilities to Justin's at the same age. But it was difficult to avoid comparing him with our friends' children. It wasn't that I was competitive; it was just so obvious that Daniel's abilities were behind those of other children his age. He wasn't behind by a few days; it was weeks and sometimes months.

The doctor was nonchalant in his assessment of Daniel. Since the growth charts allow for a broad range of what's considered normal, Daniel always fell within the range on everything. So when my friend's son, who was one day younger than Daniel, was walking on his first birthday, and Daniel was just learning to crawl, I tried to tell myself that every child is different, and I remembered that Justin hadn't started walking until almost fourteen months. All of those comforting thoughts calmed my worries for only a few minutes; I still knew that there was something wrong.

At home, Daniel was a very quiet, compliant child. He did not have many tantrums. He enjoyed playing alone, particularly with things he either could line up or stack—little toy cars, the shoes in my closet, and plastic building blocks were some of his favorite items. He loved to take baths and put on clean clothes. He did not enjoy things, however, that most kids his age would consider fun. It once took his Sunday school teacher the entire class period to get him to put his hand in plaster of paris to make a handprint for Mother's Day. Even writing or drawing in mediums such as pudding or finger paints, which most children find exciting, was like asking him to put his hands in acid—he just couldn't stand the mess.

The negative side of his behavior, however, was his screaming in the car. Even at the age of six months, he would start kicking and whining like he was trying to run away from the car as we walked toward it. We tried everything to calm him, including taking him out of the car seat to hold him, but even that method would work only temporarily. It was like something was torturing him. I began to pray and had my friends pray for Daniel to quit screaming in the car.

We moved to Houston in the fall of 1986. The move from Dallas to Houston was not nearly as traumatic as the move from Arkansas to Dallas just eighteen months earlier. We moved to a great neighborhood—I called it my "Beaver Cleaver" neighborhood. There were lots of kids, and almost all the moms stayed home. The bad part was the drive to Arkansas for a visit, which was now about seven hours instead of the four and a half hours from Dallas. No one should be subjected to the torture of listening to a child scream inconsolably for any length of time, much less seven hours in a confined area. I was not looking forward to the trip we had planned to visit my sisters and dad.

"Come on, God." I prayed silently as Daniel started screaming as we began the trip. We had driven for about forty-five minutes, and then Ron had "had it." I was trying to remain calm. I was somewhat used to Daniel's screaming, but I knew that Ron did not have as much patience—and I really couldn't blame him. He stopped the car, got out, opened the rear passenger door, looked at Daniel, and said "Stop screaming" in a pretty forceful tone. Then he shut the door, got back behind the wheel, and started driving again. Daniel looked at me and started whining like he was gearing up for round two. I just looked back at him and shook my head. He never screamed in the car again. It really was a miracle. I wish I could tell you there was some kind of formula, but there wasn't; just prayer and a firm word from Dad.

I do not want this book to be a cliché of "just pray and everything will turn out fine." In this instance, however, I firmly believe that God intervened. I don't know why he didn't intervene in other circumstances in such an immediate way, but I certainly was glad He did in this one.

CHAPTER 3

The Journey's Too Tough

*We are experiencing trouble on every side,
but are not crushed; we are perplexed, but
not driven to despair* (2 CORINTHIANS 4:8).

So many things were amazing about Daniel—his desire to be clean and dressed, his lining things up neatly, potty training! When he was around two years old, he started waking in the morning with a completely dry diaper. I had not even begun to potty train, thinking that process would be like everything else concerning Daniel's ability scale—slow. But when he consistently woke up dry, morning after morning, I thought, *Well, he's surprised me before; let's give it a try.* And as has been Daniel's pattern, which means he has no pattern, he mastered the bathroom skills better than a lot of his male peers. Maybe the fact that he didn't enjoy being dirty was a factor in that.

Yet for every accomplishment, there was a list of things that he still could not do. Talking was the biggest one. Since Justin had practically said "Thank you very much for delivering me," I was somewhat concerned that Daniel still was not saying more than a few consonant sounds by age two. He would make sounds like "cuh-cuh" for cookie or just about any word that started with the "k" sound, and "buh-buh" for Bubba, his name for Justin and "duh-duh" for Dudley, our cocker spaniel. He seemed to understand everything that was said to him, so I didn't think he had a hearing problem. Then one day, just before his second birthday, Daniel was playing in the den while Justin and I watched TV. We were engrossed in the program, not really paying attention to Daniel, when we heard him say, quite plainly, "battery." Justin and I looked at each other and then at Daniel. In his little hand was a battery that probably had fallen out of a toy. "Justin," I said, "did you just hear Daniel say the word battery?" Justin agreed that he had. We tried and tried to get Daniel to say it again, but he wouldn't. He just looked at me, gave me the battery, and went about playing. Although I was totally frustrated that he wouldn't say the word again, I had a little glimmer of hope that if he could say battery, he could say anything else. There was more in his little head than we gave him credit for having. The problem was getting what was obviously in his brain, to flow from his mouth.

The guilt that plagued me continued—guilt over the fact that I had been so sad for his first year or more of his life; guilt that I might be expecting too much; guilt that maybe I wasn't spending enough time trying to teach him, as I had with Justin. I didn't really believe any of these things, but when I couldn't find a reason for Daniel's not achieving all of the milestones he should have achieved, there was nothing left but blame and guilt. Ron was beginning to see what I had seen all along. I don't think he really noticed at first, because I was constantly compensating for Daniel and just not talking about my fears or apprehensions. But when our friends' children, who were all within weeks of the same age as Daniel, were moving forward much more quickly, it became so obvious that I couldn't hide it anymore. I knew I had to get a doctor to believe me when I'd say that I didn't care if Daniel was "on the chart": there was something wrong. And finally, one did.

Daniel was a healthy child, other than having an intestinal parasite called *Giardia* when he was eighteen months old and a few ear infections, so we mostly went to the doctor for well checkups. It was just before his third birthday when we were getting ready to move back to Dallas, and I wanted our pediatrician to see him for his three-year well-check before we moved. I voiced my concerns over Daniel's inability (or lack of desire) to talk. I described it like this: "It's as if he has a short in the wiring of his brain. Sometimes the wires touch and a light comes on." I just thought we needed to find the "wire" and fix it. The pediatrician suggested we see an ear, nose, and throat (ENT) doctor for a possible hearing test. While I thought this was a waste of time, it was the first time a doctor had given me any inkling that he believed what I was saying, so we went to the ENT.

As I suspected, Daniel did not have a hearing problem. He'd had multiple ear infections as a baby, but none of those had caused any permanent damage. The ENT suggested that we find a speech therapist once we got to Dallas. *Thank goodness*—I was so relieved to have a direction.

I still don't understand our little sojourn in Houston, because we only lived there a little over a year. Ron's old boss, Richard Lewis, from Murphy Oil, had moved to Houston shortly after we moved to Dallas. Once Richard settled in his new job at Anadarko Petroleum, he asked Ron to come to Houston work with him in the benefits department. We loved Houston and quickly had found a home in a neighborhood north of Houston called Kingwood. We soon had a new church and friends so when Ron told me that some businessmen, with whom he had been working before we moved to Houston, had started a new trust company and wanted him as president and head of sales, my emotions were somewhat torn. It was a huge promotion for him with potential for growth and expansion. He was entering a new venture, not only with this company but also in his responsibilities. Ron would be responsible for the day-to-day business, as well as acquiring new clients and growing the company. It was very exciting but again, stressful for all of us as well as a little sad to leave our new friends in Kingwood. I was happy at least that we were moving back to our friends in Dallas and could just slide right back into the life we had left only the year before.

Once the new company was up and running, I met the other partners. Coincidentally, one of them had a daughter who was a speech therapist. Her name was Mary Ellen, and she became our savior. As soon as we were settled into our home, we started going to Miss Mary Ellen's house three days a week. Daniel loved it. She had a huge playroom, where her three girls had every kind of toy known to man. Daniel quickly understood that if he followed what Mary Ellen wanted to do, he got to spend the last few minutes of his visit in this virtual Santa's workshop. Mary Ellen was very encouraging and showed special affection for Daniel. He never balked at going to speech, which was wonderful. She gave us assignments each week, and one book, in particular, became our constant companion. It was a picture book with three-word sentences that we would read over and over, so that Daniel would get the rhythm of saying words together. It took a whole year but Daniel finally began speaking in full sentences. At first, it was just three or four words strung together, but it definitely was a sentence. He quickly moved on to lengthy sentences, with words he shouldn't have been able to articulate and used in the correct context. For the first time, I could hear him arguing with Justin, playing make-believe with his plastic building blocks, or just talking in general. Since then, he has never stopped.

After a year of speech therapy, Mary Ellen told us that Daniel no longer needed her services. While we would miss Mary Ellen, I was happy that we didn't have to spend two hours (including drive time), three days a week, on private speech therapy—not to mention that insurance hadn't covered it. We were all so happy that Daniel was communicating so well. I tried to think, *Whew! Okay, that's done. Now we can just move on like a normal family.* But speech was not Daniel's only issue. He could walk, run, and talk, but his fine motor skills were so delayed that drawing, coloring, or cutting with scissors were just torture for him. I enrolled Daniel in a two-days-a-week preschool for three-year-olds. His birthday is in January, so he was one of the older kids in the class, yet he was so far behind in fine motor abilities that his teacher did a lot of his work for him.

His teacher very kindly talked to me about possibly helping Daniel at home with his use of scissors. Guilt overwhelmed me again. I had to admit that cutting with scissors was not an activity on which I'd spent much time. I had tried to teach him his alphabet and to sit quietly while I read a book or when he colored in a coloring book—all the things that I did with Justin and that Justin had loved. These were not things, however, that Daniel loved, so I found myself not spending as much time doing them. But as suggested, we got the scissors and a newspaper and sat in the floor, hour after hour, cutting strips of paper. Scissors never were something I could say he mastered.

By this time, we knew for sure that Daniel was left-handed. I had noticed it long before he should have preferred one hand to the other. Even as an infant, he reached, pulled, and manipulated more with his left hand. Now, doctors will tell you that when a baby favors one hand over the other before, say, age two or three, there's probably a reason. I didn't know that then, however, even though I thought it was unusual. This fact is something I probably should have mentioned to the doctor, but I just didn't think it was significant.

Being left-handed in a right-handed world is obstacle enough, but add to that a difficulty with fine motor skills, and you have a real challenge. Teaching Daniel to button his own shirt, tie his shoes, or even use a zipper was difficult. We opted mostly for pants without snaps, buttons, or zippers, such as sweatpants, and for shoes that didn't need tying, such as hook-and-loop strapped shoes. These items gave him a sense of being able to do things by himself. I knew that he eventually would have to tackle the buttons, shoestrings, and such, but for now, we were happy with getting clothes on and shoes on the correct feet.

By age six, though, when most children are relatively proficient at getting themselves dressed in all manner of clothing, Daniel still was learning these basic procedures. I tried for weeks to teach him to tie his shoes. Daniel knew that all of his friends could tie their own shoes. He was frustrated with himself because he just couldn't do it. He was tired of being different by wearing the strap-on shoes. He wanted lace-up shoes more than anything. So we took on the new challenge of shoelace tying. We worked and worked. I taught myself how to tie backward from my normal right-handed procedure, so that I could teach Daniel more easily. Nothing helped. He just couldn't manipulate the strings and the loop, and he hated using the "send the bunny through the hole" analogy. He thought that sounded babyish. He just wanted to learn to tie his shoes—period.

One day, Ron's aunt Patty came to visit when we were in the middle of a tying lesson. Aunt Patty is left-handed, so she said, "Let me see if I can help." She sat down with Daniel, and within five minutes, he was tying his shoes. I was in shock. I said, "Show me what you did. I've been trying to teach him for weeks." When she showed me the process that she'd taught him, I laughed out loud. I evidently always tied my shoes left-handed without realizing it. So when I reversed my way of tying shoes, trying to help my left-handed child, I'd unwittingly changed it to a right-handed method. Once Aunt Patty showed Daniel the correct left-handed way, he got it! What a thrill it was to watch him tie his own shoes, over and over again. *Another accomplishment! Can we be done now?* I wondered. Oh, but we had only just begun.

CHAPTER 4

When "They" Look in Your Eyes

"For I know the plans I have for you,"
declares the Lord, "plans to prosper you
and not to harm you, plans to give you
hope and a future" (JEREMIAH 29:11).

With each milestone accomplished, I would comfort myself with "Maybe now we can be 'normal.'" But it still was not to be. Daniel was about to begin kindergarten. Justin was attending a private school associated with our church, so naturally we wanted Daniel to attend there as well. The great thing, we thought, was that the person who would be Daniel's kindergarten teacher had been his Sunday school teacher for the past year. She knew and loved Daniel. I voiced my concerns to her about Daniel's abilities and what I considered his disabilities. I told her I did not think he could keep pace with the other students. I knew that this private school prided itself (as most private schools do) on moving quickly and being ahead of the public schools and other private schools.

We already had scheduled an IQ test at Scottish Rite Hospital for Children soon after Daniel turned five years old—Mary Ellen had suggested this when Daniel was taking speech from her, saying it was our best course of action. She had told us there was no hurry to give him an IQ test, but that we might want to do it before he started school, just so he could get the best help, if necessary. We were on the waiting list at Scottish Rite for seven months. He would take the test just before school started, but the results would not be available until after school was in session.

I have never been so nervous about a test. This was an *intelligence* test. While I hated to think Daniel had an intelligence issue, I didn't know how he would score on a standardized test. He was not one to enjoy sitting down to do workbook material, so I was afraid his attention span would be his downfall. I was right.

Daniel started kindergarten that fall and, as I predicted, quickly fell behind his fellow students. His teacher had a look of concern on her face each day when I picked Daniel up from school. Having Daniel in Sunday school was nothing like having him in class on a daily basis. Sunday school is about listening to a story from the Bible while sitting in a circle and then coloring a page about the story. No one cared how you colored a page in Sunday school. As long as you were quiet during story time and bowed your head during prayer time, drank your juice, and ate your cookies, all was good in Sunday school. But this was real school—the place where people expected a certain level of performance. By the time the scores from Scottish Rite were available, I already saw the handwriting on the chalkboard, so to speak.

As predicted, Daniel's scores from Scottish Rite were abysmal. The woman who had given Daniel the test and who now was assigned to give us the "bad" news was visibly upset. She said, "I know these scores appear very low, and they are, but I know that Daniel is not the person on this form. However, I had to score him according to his first response or if he did not respond at all." According to his score, he would be considered "educable mentally retarded." which meant Daniel should not be able to communicate verbally very well; he should not be able to dress himself or even be aware of his surroundings—all of which Daniel could do. The diagnostician assured me that the scores on this test did not reflect the child she saw sitting in front of her. Her assurances were meant to be comforting, but only lasted about five minutes, because I knew that she had to send those scores to our school. She suggested we bring Daniel back in a couple of years to retake the test and that we should make an appointment with a children's neurologist for a second opinion. I left the meeting nodding my head, as if I understood, but felt like someone had pulled a dark cloud down over my head.

Unfortunately, the recommendations and opinions of the diagnostician did not help when it came to talking to the administration of the school about Daniel's ability— or inability, as it were. Once the school got the scores, someone in administration at the school called Ron to talk about Daniel. As they discussed Daniel's testing and a possible next step, the person said something that hit Ron like a ton of bricks—and it has never left his heart since: "Ron, you and Lisa need to realize that Daniel just does not have the gray matter that it takes to stay at our school."

Ron wanted to reach through the phone, grab the administrator by the throat, and scream, *"Gray matter?"* Instead, he calmly and without emotion asked for suggestions on what to do.

The school recommended strongly that we put Daniel in special education classes elsewhere—but this was more than a recommendation; it was mandatory. Daniel could not stay at the school beyond the six weeks report card period, which would conclude in about one week from that date.

We were totally floored and overwhelmed. We had no idea how to even begin finding the best educational program for Daniel. We had been committed to our children having Christian education, but that looked like it was going to be impossible for Daniel. The headmaster's secretary gave me some names of private schools for kids with learning disabilities, and I went down the list, calling for interviews. The challenge was threefold: school was already in session and most classes were full; the tuition for these special schools was two or three times what we were paying for private school; and there were no Christian schools for students with learning disabilities. To further complicate matters, Ron traveled for his job about 70 percent of the time, so for me to get Justin to his school in downtown Dallas and then get Daniel to a different school, especially considering Dallas traffic, seemed logistically and physically impossible. But we had no choice. Amazingly, we found a school within that seven-day period that made an opening for Daniel. Since there were no Christian schools for kids with learning disabilities, we settled for a small private school called Oak Hill Academy. The staff was very caring and sweet. The children were in small, Montessori-style classrooms. Daniel did well with the transition. He was enrolled in the preschool class, as the kindergarten class was full, but the teachers assured me that they would "catch him up" as soon as possible and that he would never know the difference after a year or so.

We followed the suggestion of the test administrator at Scottish Rite and found a children's neurologist for Daniel. After several hours of testing and several weeks of waiting on results, we were called for our follow-up appointment. Although Daniel was not diagnosed as "educable mentally retarded," the name for his diagnosis didn't seem much better: pervasive developmental disorder—Not Otherwise Specified, or PDD-NOS.

The best way I can explain what a diagnosis of PDD-NOS means is to equate it to going to the doctor when you just don't feel well. You're achy, feverish, and tired, and the doctor tells you that you have a virus. Having a virus means there's nothing the doctor can do for you, except to tell you to go home, rest, drink plenty of fluids, and call if you're not better in a week or so. That's what a diagnosis of PDD-NOS is like. Pervasive means "to become spread throughout all parts," which meant that Daniel's mind and body were affected in some way by a disability with no real name—"not otherwise specified".

And further, there was nothing anyone could do about it. We were told not to expect him to do the normal things of childhood, like riding a bike, skating, or playing organized sports. This translated into the future as "no driving, college, or meaningful occupation."

The word autism was never mentioned at any of our neurologist appointments. In the early nineties, autism was still a rare diagnosis. I had only heard the word from the movie "Rainman" and since Daniel didn't behave like the character played by Dustin Hoffman, autism never crossed my mind. Apparently, it didn't cross the doctors' minds either or at least they never said it out loud nor did they write it in their reports. Today we know that autism has many characteristics including PDD-NOS.

I don't like to openly confront anyone, although I will be defiant silently. So when the doctor told me what *not* to expect, I felt my defiance taking over. I nodded my head as if I understood his words, even though my mind was screaming, "Watch me!" I immediately set out to prove the doctors wrong. One of the first things we did was buy Daniel a bicycle, even though he had not mastered even riding a tricycle—pedaling and steering at the same time was quite a challenge. Pedaling itself was difficult. For some reason, his little feet would not stay on the pedals and go round and round. They would go back and forth, which meant he never went anywhere. This became quite monotonous after a while so he was not interested in riding his tricycle.

I devised a plan. His two-wheeled bike had training wheels that I propped up on bricks, so that the back wheel did not touch the ground. Then I got behind the bike and held Daniel's feet on the pedals as they went round and round. We did this exercise for several days until he could keep his feet on the pedals. Then we practiced pushing backward on the pedals to feel the brake. *Talk about confusing*, I thought. *Finally, he gets the forward pedaling, and now I'm telling him to push backward.* But after about a week of doing this exercise, he was ready to try it on the ground. We started in the grass so that if (when) he fell, it wouldn't be too traumatic. Then we practiced in the driveway and finally on the sidewalk. It took a couple of weeks, but Daniel learned to ride a bicycle! It didn't take long before he even wanted to take off the training wheels. Bike riding remained one of his favorite activities for a long time.

After accomplishing such a monumental activity, the other activities that the doctor had told us not to try were just a matter of desire and trial. He wanted to learn to Rollerblade, so we got him a pair of inline skates. He became so adept at skating that he played roller hockey for one season and always enjoyed a game of street hockey with his brother. It was the team sports part of roller hockey that was difficult, not the skating.

When someone looks you in the eyes and tells you what *not* to expect, don't just accept it. See for yourself what your child can accomplish. You will occasionally be disappointed, but mostly, you will be amazed.

CHAPTER 5

An Indefinite Time

Hope deferred makes the heart sick, but a longing fulfilled is like a tree of life.
(PROVERBS 13:12)

Time is relative. We can say we have no time to do something, when of course, we have the same amount of time in each day as anyone else. When we say something lasted a long time, we are comparing it to what we determine is a short time. For instance, if I say I was sick for a long time, I could mean that I had the flu for a week. That would be a long time for me, as I've never been sick for more than a week. But for someone else who says "I was sick for a long time," it could mean they had a disease or chronic illness for many years. But when we think of an indefinite time, we assume a time frame that is possibly without end. So we attempt to live each day to create meaning, to create significance, so that our time here on earth will not be in vain.

I heard a quote recently: "We don't waste time. We waste ourselves." I think finding meaning to life and to our time on earth is why the story that our guest speaker told that Sunday (that I mentioned in the introduction) meant so much to me. When she told that her husband would have said yes to a daughter, even if God had told him he could only have her for six years, it really made me think about time and how unmerciful and limited it really is.

When a child receives the diagnosis of any kind of physical or mental challenge, time again becomes unmerciful. There is no end to the challenge facing him or her—or you. There will be battles won but many more lost. With Daniel, teaching him to tie his shoes, button his shirt, and ride a bike were all things that came with time and a lot of practice. But there were some things that time would not allow. There is not enough time to teach him everything he possibly needs to know so that he can understand why some people would not accept him as their friend. There is not enough time to teach him why he can't go to the same school as his brother and sister. There's not enough time to figure out what to do that will be best for all concerned. There's never enough time.

Thankfully, Daniel's disability has been an advantage many times. Because he doesn't read cues very well, he often doesn't realize when someone is ignoring him or being mean. But there were occasions when the cruelty of other children (and by default, their parents) was too blatant to ignore. For several summers, I served as a counselor at our church's youth camp. I was the cabin mom for ninth-grade girls. Because I had a cabin to myself, situated between the two girls' cabins, I could bring Justin and Daniel to camp, and they could stay in the cabin with me. They loved it. We brought their bicycles and bathing suits and lots of bug spray, and they were free to roam the camp pretty much as they pleased. Other counselors brought their children as well, so for a week, they were able to taste a freedom similar to my own when I was growing up—get on their bikes after breakfast, play with their friends, come in for lunch, go back out to swim or play again, and then in for dinner. As long as Justin was with Daniel, everything went well. I knew that Justin would protect Daniel and make sure he was included.

The problem came when Justin had to go home one day to play in a baseball game. Daniel was left on his own for the day while I spent time with the girls. As usual, it didn't take long for the other boys to realize that Daniel didn't have his protector with him. I saw Daniel standing alone, looking into the woods near the lunchroom. I asked him what he was doing, and he explained that the boys had created a club but would not allow him to join. Before the boys realized I was standing behind Daniel, I heard every unkind, malicious word they said to Daniel. I called them out and took them to their mothers. There was an apology of sorts to Daniel, but nothing changed in their behavior as far as including Daniel. You might think the boys were just being kids, and I probably would have said the same thing—before Daniel came along. I guess it's different when it's someone you love who's taking the brunt of the hateful talk. Nonetheless, I didn't think I could subject Daniel to that type of "socializing" again. It was our last year to go to camp.

While Daniel may have been less than perceptive in many ways, he was very perceptive in others. A friend of mine told me once that she was always nervous when Daniel came to her house because he could find a picture that was crooked or a book out of place on the shelf and tell her it needed to be corrected. He had a photographic memory and this ability came in handy when we couldn't find an item we had misplaced, for instance, keys, a hairbrush, or shoes. If Daniel had seen it, he could tell us where it was. We called him "the finder".

Another way he was perceptive regarded changes in routine. In 1992, we had another child, Allie Beth. It was exciting to have a baby sister in the house but also a huge adjustment. Justin and Daniel were ten and seven, respectively, when Allie was born, so they had been used to picking up and going anywhere at a moment's notice. If we wanted to go to a movie in the middle of day, we went. If we wanted to go the water park three times in one week, we went. Now, with a baby in the house, all that changed. When Allie Beth was about four months old, and the boys asked one day if we could go to a movie, I had to explain that Allie needed a nap, and we would need at least an hour to get ready after that, and by that time, the movie would be over. Daniel sighed and said, "Mom, remember when it was just us?" I gave my best understanding smile and said, "Yes, Daniel, I remember."

In January 1993, we decided to start looking for a new home. We were living in Dallas in an older neighborhood, which we liked, but there were not a lot of kids or a safe place for the boys to ride their bikes or Rollerblade. We moved north to Mckinney, but because the drive to Oak Hill Academy and to Justin's school would be too far, we had to make some changes. Justin was going into sixth grade and began attending a Christian school in North Dallas. It was still a long drive, but not nearly as far as driving to downtown Dallas, and we had the advantage of carpooling with other families in McKinney whose children went to the same school.

Even though we knew the probable answer, we talked to the administration about enrolling Daniel in the same school as Justin. We were willing to pay an extra fee for special tutoring, but the administration didn't feel that they could offer what Daniel needed. While we understood logically, it was none-the-less disappointing. Lest it sounds like only Christian schools would not accept Daniel as a student, we also tried to enroll Daniel in a private school that was nearby for children with learning differences, but once again after seeing his test scores, they would not admit him. I begged them to just visit with Daniel-to not just look at a number, but look at this child. They would not, so we decided to homeschool him.

Allie Beth was eighteen months old when we started homeschooling Daniel. While I am not a proponent of using TV as a babysitter, I was thankful for the purple dinosaur and lamb puppet that were on public television at the time—when you have a child like Daniel who has to have undivided attention for an extended period of time, you take what you can get. On Tuesdays and Thursdays, I had Mother's Day Out preschool program for Allie, at a local church but on Monday, Wednesday, and Friday, we had public-television characters to keep her occupied. Obviously, our school sessions were not always productive. Allie Beth loved learning, so many times, she would sit in on our home school sessions. I knew we had a problem when after a couple of years, she began to answer the questions and read some of the words that I was trying to teach Daniel. Daniel knew it, too. He recognized that Allie, even as a toddler, was able to learn some of the things he was being taught. He did not like her in our "classroom." It was not long before he started asking to go to "real school" again.

Back then, the Internet wasn't as available for research as it is today, so I dragged out the Yellow Pages and again started looking for a school for Daniel. *Can there be a school that will teach Christian values and academics for kids with learning differences?* I wondered. After calling, visiting, and driving by several schools, I found one that I thought would be right for Daniel—Keystone Academy. It was a relatively new school and was billed as a Christian school for students with learning differences. *Wow!* I thought. *Finally!*

I let Daniel go to school half-days for one week, just to see how he would do. He loved it and asked if he could go all day. I was so happy. It was an answer to my prayer. We enjoyed our time at Keystone. I became very involved as a room mother and helped with every event that I could. I wanted to make sure that Daniel's educational needs were being met, but more than that, I wanted to be able to watch him grow socially. He was making friends for the first time, and that was so great.

Close to the end of fifth grade, I had a conference with the principal and Daniel's teacher, whose degree was in special education. They sat across from me and explained that Daniel had reached his capacity for learning. He would never advance, they said, beyond fifth grade. I looked at them incredulously and said, "So you're telling me that he is incapable of learning beyond what you have taught him to this point?" They nodded their heads sadly. I said, "Well, obviously, he will not learn anything else here." Daniel was homeschooled again for sixth grade.

Again, after homeschooling for sixth grade, Daniel was interested in going back to school—every time we homeschooled, he wanted to go to "real" school. My feelings might have been hurt, but they weren't; I was happy that he had such persistence and a resistance to the frustration (and sometimes emotional pain) that came with school environments. We found another school for seventh and eighth grades, a small school run by a mother-and-daughter team. They were very sweet and seemed to have such open hearts for kids with learning differences. I felt that Daniel would be safe at this school, and with small classrooms, he would be able to move forward with learning as well.

Seventh grade went pretty well. There were a few incidents on the playground with some older boys, but these were mostly just boys being aggressive while playing soccer or some other sport involving a ball. Daniel is not an aggressive person, but the teacher said I was going to have to instruct Daniel to defend himself. I said that I would be thrilled if Daniel would stand up to these boys, but that was not in Daniel's nature. No amount of cajoling would change that fact.

By the end of eighth grade, Daniel felt like he had at least one friend. I was happy that he felt that way. One friend was great. About two weeks before school was out for that year, we were home, having just finished dinner. I was at the kitchen sink, washing dishes, when the phone rang. Daniel answered it and seemed happy that it was for him, which was rare. His friend from school was calling, which never had happened. The boy lived about an hour outside the Dallas city limits, so getting together for after-school friend-building time was not a possibility. After about a minute on the phone, Daniel's tone of voice changed. I looked at him and saw that his cheeks were flushed. He looked at me with alarm or shock. He kept saying, "I don't know why you're saying that stuff." I told him to hang up the phone. When he got off the phone, he was visibly shaken. At first, Daniel wouldn't tell me what the boy had said. He was too embarrassed. Finally, he said the boy had made comments about what he and Daniel could do together sexually or what Daniel could do by himself. I was now the one who was shaken.

I immediately called the school and left a message, and when the headmistress called back, I explained what had happened. There was no question in her mind that Daniel was telling the truth. I learned that this boy had had several run-ins with the law by age thirteen. She tried to assure me that she would discipline the child and even had the boy's mother call me. The mother apologized for her son, and I was sympathetic to her, but I couldn't let Daniel be subjected to the boy's behavior. Thankfully, that school did not have grades past the eighth grade, so we needed to find another school for ninth grade anyway. Unfortunately, the social situation at the next school wasn't much better.

Again, the new school's owners were upstanding and caring, but by the time children with learning disabilities and/or autism reach high school, they have undergone a lot of trauma just to get through the educational processes, not to mention bullying and social issues. Often, there are a lot of broken children who become broken young adults who hurt because they've been hurt. They find social groups where they will be accepted and those groups are often unhealthy physically, mentally and emotionally. When I heard one mom at a parents' meeting say, "I'm just glad my child doesn't pull a knife on me anymore," I knew we were not going to stay at this school long term.

CHAPTER 6

God, Please Just Fix It

Jesus answered, "Neither this man nor his parents sinned, but he was born blind so that the acts of God may be revealed through what happens to him" (JOHN 9:3).

I remember thinking, *After the year we lived through in 1985 and our struggles with Daniel, surely my share of bad stuff is over.* I know. There's no quota on good or bad that can happen in one's lifetime, but I sort of held on to that thought like a good-luck charm. God says he won't give us more than we can handle, right?

I don't remember how we found our speech therapist in McKinney, Sally Bober, but she was a godsend. She specialized in adult-care speech therapy for stroke victims, but she agreed to take Daniel as a client. She was just beginning to practice a therapy called sensory integration. I was excited about the studies she mentioned of patients who had made remarkable progress after just a few sessions.

Daniel would be one of her first patients for this type of therapy. Sally used one technique that we had done, quite by accident, since Daniel was very little. It was called *deep pressure*. Daniel loved to be held tightly. When he was still an infant, he would bury his head in the side of my neck while I rocked him. He seemed to want to crawl inside of me to get closer. He also loved thick, heavy clothing, like fleece pants and shirts. He had a favorite set of clothes that I often washed three or four times a week so he could wear them again. He loved stuffing toys and other objects into the pant legs. We often would hear Daniel clanking down the hall, and once I kept hearing a bell ring every time he walked. I finally said, "Daniel, what do you have in your pants that keeps ringing?" He reached in and pulled out an entire telephone—not a toy phone but an actual phone that we no longer used.

The layered look, I'm convinced, was inspired by Daniel. He was layering his clothing before layering was cool. He hardly ever went without wearing at least two shirts at any time. So "deep pressure" on his little body was something that obviously was important to him. Sally taught us to use this therapy in a meaningful way. Daniel loved it. To this day, one of his favorite things to do is get a massage.

I wish I could say that sensory integration massaged our problems away, but the lessons continued. In 1995, our oldest son, Justin, was on the junior varsity football team in high school, which played on Thursday nights. He took a pretty good hit one night, face mask to face mask. He had his "bell rung," as the coach would say. He didn't pass out but definitely felt the effects of the hit for several minutes. He got home late that Thursday night, overslept on Friday morning, and ran out the door to catch his ride without having breakfast. He had several tests that day, so by the time he sat down for lunch, I guess his body said "no more"—it convulsed in a seizure. He had never had a seizure, nor had anyone in our family. The school called an ambulance and then notified us so we could meet it at the hospital. The doctors said the seizure was probably from a concussion from the night before, and it was a one-time thing.

We took Justin home and everything seemed fine. Six weeks later, he was playing basketball with a friend in a driveway down the street. This time, he sensed something was wrong—it's what doctors call an "aura"; a feeling that can't really be explained but which is common in people with epilepsy. He was able to walk home and tell his grandmother that he felt funny, just before he fell on the floor in another grand mal seizure. Ron and I were at a business meeting downtown when we got this call. Again, we went to the hospital, but now, because Justin had had two seizures, they called it epilepsy. He was immediately put on medication.

We felt lucky that the first medication we tried took care of Justin's seizures. And knowing what we know now, we *were* lucky. Four years later, Allie Beth was walking past Daniel's bedroom to go downstairs when she yelled, "Mom, there's something wrong with Daniel." She had seen Justin have his second seizure and even though she was only three years old, it was a vivid memory for her. This was the same scene she witnessed in Daniel's room that morning. I ran to his room and found him on the floor having a grand mal seizure. I was somewhat in shock, but thankfully, my mother-in-law was there, and she helped me call 911. The ambulance came and took Daniel to the hospital.

After doing the normal tests, CT scans, blood work, and other tests, the doctors determined that Daniel's seizure was a fluke. There was no reason for Daniel to have had a seizure. He had not hit his head, taken drugs, or done anything to cause a seizure. We were sent home, just as we had been with Justin. About nine months later, it happened again—almost the same scenario: early morning, falls out of the bed, call 911, go to the hospital, run the same tests. Daniel was placed on the same anti-seizure medication as Justin had been given, but we were not so lucky this time. The medicine that had worked so well for Justin had a negative effect on Daniel, giving him a rash that would not go away. The doctor decided to change the medication. It wouldn't be the only time.

About six months later, Justin had graduated from high school and was now attending Samford University in Birmingham, Alabama. Ron decided to drive to Birmingham to take Daniel to visit Justin. They stopped at my sister's house in El Dorado to spend the night before continuing the ten-hour trip. While there, Daniel had a seizure unlike those he'd previously experienced. This time, he just stared into space and slumped or fell to the floor. There was no shaking or anything typical of a grand mal seizure. Ron took him to the hospital, where he had the same protocol of blood work, CT scan, and observation. Since Ron and Daniel were out of town, it was decided to increase the dosage of Daniel's current medicines until he could see his regular neurologist. The seizures happened frequently on the trip, and we had no idea what we were in for on their return.

Once Daniel was back in Dallas, we of course went to see his neurologist. This time, the doctor added an additional drug to the one he was taking. We were told to expect the drug to take effect in a few days. Unfortunately, we noticed nothing except increased seizures. This started us on the roller-coaster ride that was the drug-of-the-week program—we weren't actually on a different drug every week, but it sure seemed like it. After about six months, instead of having one or two seizures a day, Daniel was having one or two *per hour.* Someone had to stand beside him at all times in case he fell. It was like watching a five-foot-nine, 160-pound two-year-old. We had to make sure he wasn't standing next to something that would injure him if he should fall. We eventually just made him sit as much as possible, so that if he had a seizure, he would just slump to one side but would not hurt himself. It was a traumatic time for all of us.

We were very fortunate that Daniel never had a serious accident from his falls—mostly scrapes and bruises. Once, though, he fell in the shower and hit his head on the spout, which required about seven stitches.

By this time, Daniel was in tenth grade, and we had decided to homeschool yet again. This time, we hired a tutor for math and science, and I only taught English. That's about all we could handle. We also had a personal trainer come to our house three days a week so that Daniel could get some exercise. Obviously, going out to play ball or going to a gym was out of the question. This home-school setup was working for the most part, but I knew that Daniel was not completely happy with the situation.

In the summer of 2002, Justin was home from college, Allie Beth had finished fourth grade, and Daniel and I had completed tenth grade—I felt like I completed each grade as Daniel completed it. Even when we were not homeschooling, I was "re-teaching" Daniel every night with homework or supplemental work. On one particular hot July day, I was sitting outside while Daniel swam in the pool. I had to keep a sharp eye on him, because he still was having seizures, but we felt we couldn't just put him in a bubble, so we tried to allow him to have as much freedom and normalcy as possible. Daniel swam over to the side of the pool and, with tears in his eyes, said, "Mom, I really want to go to school." I wanted so badly to say "No! We are not trying school again."

I had long since given up the notion of Daniel getting a Christian education. I was just hoping for some type of completion of school at this point. I told him I would see what I could do, but it probably would mean public school. He was okay with that. He told me he just wanted to be part of a team. Daniel didn't mean that in a sports-team sense; he just wanted to feel part of something bigger than himself. He wanted to have a reason to cheer for something and have a group identity.

At first, I searched schools for children with learning disabilities. The only ones I found were those we either had attended already or had tried to attend and were turned away, so I started the process of enrolling him in the public school. Our only experience with public schools had been the two times we had used the speech and occupational therapy that was available to us through the Americans with Disabilities Act. All public schools must allow access to therapies or any service for any child in need of those services in their school district. The experience we had with both of the public school situations had not been ideal. It was hardly enough therapy to make a dent in Daniel's abilities, but we accepted what we could get. Unfortunately, because of Daniel's varied educational experience, other than the tests that he had taken through Scottish Rite and the neurologist, we couldn't give the schools much to assess where they should place Daniel. The solution the public school gave me was to put him in a general education class for ninth grade while they assessed and tested him. This process could take about six weeks. I responded that I didn't think that was a good idea, as Daniel was already sixteen years old. I knew that he would feel awkward in a classroom of fourteen-year-old freshmen. I also felt that if I were the mother of a fourteen-year-old freshman, I would not want a nearly seventeen-year-old young man in the same class as my child. They told me there was no other option. I kept Daniel on the enrollment list but continued my search.

I'm not sure what words I put in the computer search engine on this particular day, but the name of a Christian school popped up. I thought it must be a mistake, but I looked at their website. Liberty Christian School was a college preparatory, Christian school, but they had added a program for high school students with learning disabilities. I thought it was probably similar to other

Christian schools with a learning lab where students went for extra help or to take tests when they needed extra time. But as I read, I became more intrigued and hopeful.

We were already at the end of July, and I knew the chance of a private school having any room left for a new student was going to be slim. The only reason I called Liberty was because I had promised Daniel I would do everything I could to find a school for him to attend. No one answered the phone the day I called. July typically is the month that schools have the fewest employees on campus. I left a message but didn't expect a return call until sometime in August.

The next day I received a phone call from the headmaster of Liberty Christian School, Rodney Haire. He didn't know if they had space available in the program for students with learning disabilities, but he gave my name to the woman in charge of the program. A few hours later, Melanie Davis called to talk to me about her program at Liberty. As she explained the way they proposed to work with and help students with learning differences. I was amazed. Could a typical Christian school (or private school, for that matter) really want to help every child learn in the best way possible? From what Melanie described, it certainly sounded as if Liberty did. We set an appointment to have Daniel tested (that dreaded word) and to talk with the headmaster.

Ron and I drove up to Denton, Texas, where Liberty was located, about thirty miles from our house in Dallas. We didn't tell Daniel what we were doing, because I didn't want him to be disappointed if this interview didn't go well. Mr. Haire was very sympathetic to our story of educational woe. He didn't know a lot about learning disabilities, but regardless, our story touched him, and he felt that, for Daniel, this was more about "throwing out a lifeline," as he put it, than just getting an education. Daniel was scheduled for testing the next day.

As was par for the course, Daniel's test results were not good. But God, in His mercy, led Mr. Haire to give Daniel the opportunity to go to Liberty anyway. The only problem was that the program was full at that moment. There was only space for six students per therapist; currently, there were two therapists, and every slot was full. They were looking for a third therapist so that they could add more students, but they had not found one. When Ron and I walked out to the car, I could already feel what had to be done, and I knew that Ron was going to say the same thing: "You have to be the therapist." I certainly had not gone to this interview for a job, but at the same time, I knew that it was the only way I could fulfill my promise to Daniel to do everything I could to find him a school.

My heart was breaking, because I knew this would mean a huge sacrifice for our family—everyone was so used to my not working outside the home, especially Allie Beth. This meant that Ron or his mom would need to take Allie to school and pick her up. (I could not have done any of this if my mother-in-law, Dorothy Simmons, had not been so willing to do whatever it took to help us out. She lived with us for almost twenty years, and there was nothing she wouldn't do to make sure all of our children were cared for, sometimes at great inconvenience to her.

To this day, she is our biggest cheerleader.) My working outside the home also would mean that I could not be as involved with Allie Beth's school activities as I always had been. I cried for a couple of weeks after beginning my position at Liberty; it was devastating to me. I was thrust into a super-fast training session to learn about a therapy with which I had been completely unfamiliar two weeks earlier, while my heart was yearning to go back to my comfort zone of home.

Daniel still was having seizures several times a day. After a while, the students and teachers stopped running to get me every time he fell or slumped over. They learned to let him get up on his own and keep going. Daniel never remembered having the seizures, so he would just get up, dust himself off, get his bearings, and go to class. It was quite remarkable to watch but heartbreaking at the same time.

After the first week of school, I was exhausted emotionally and physically. Ron said that he would take Daniel to the first home football game at Liberty that Friday night. Friday nights in Texas in autumn are very exciting! I've always loved going to high school football games, even though I know next to nothing about the game itself. There's nothing like being under those bright stadium lights with excited, cheering fans. I did not go to this first game, however, but I wish I had. Ron told me later that when they walked into the stadium, Daniel looked up at the lights and said, "Finally, a team!" That's what he had wanted all along—a team he could call his own. He wasn't on the football team, of course, but he knew that he was part of something bigger, and in that sense, he was part of the team. He was a Liberty Christian Warrior. Nothing could have been truer. To this day, it is one of the most touching moments for Ron and me to recount.

The therapy sessions that had drawn us to Liberty did not accomplish all we had hoped for Daniel's learning ability, but he did finish school at Liberty Christian in May 2004. We were so happy to watch him be part of his class on that stage, wearing a cap and gown. He walked across as proud as if he had been valedictorian. In our hearts, he *was* valedictorian. He had proven that if you set your heart and mind on something and keep pursuing it with all your might, you will achieve it. Maybe the results won't be exactly what was planned or hoped for, but it will be God's best for you. Ron gave the commencement speech that day, "Are You a Participant or a Crusader?" It was an incredible way to finish our educational experience . . . as crusaders!

CHAPTER 7

His Smile Will Bring Joy

A happy heart makes the face cheerful, but heartache crushes the spirit (Proverbs 15:13).

Many characteristics are considered typical of people with autism. Because there is such a wide array of symptoms, these general characteristics now are more commonly referred to as a "spectrum." Some people with autism are totally nonverbal, only making noises that are seemingly random and noncommunicative. Other people on the spectrum are very verbal; in fact, they may be more verbal than their neurotypical peers, often using very advanced terms and descriptions in their everyday language. Unfortunately, many times they are just as dysfunctional in their communication skills as the nonverbal person on the spectrum, because what they want to communicate either is uninteresting to others or they are so focused on their subject of interest that they cannot intertwine their conversation with what may be going on around them.

Daniel's verbal skills, once he acquired them, were on par with his peers and, at times, quite advanced. Occasionally, he did obsess on certain topics. For instance, when he was about four years old, the Teenage Mutant Ninja Turtles cartoon characters were all the rage. He became obsessed with the TV show and all of the paraphernalia associated with the characters—Raphael, Leonardo, Michelangelo, and Donatello. I had tried to teach Daniel his alphabet, just as I had Justin, from a very early age. Daniel, however, could not remember most of the letters—but he knew that "R" was for Raphael, "L" was for Leonardo, "M" was for Michelangelo, "D" was for Donatello (and Daniel), and "A" was for April (the heroine of the series).

Daniel was so fascinated by this group of ninja fighters that he called himself Turtle for at least a year. His Sunday school teacher stopped me one day after class and asked me again what his name was, because the only name he would give her was "Turtle." All of the children called him Turtle, even though I signed him into class each week as Daniel. I don't remember when he stopped calling himself Turtle, but he finally did. I was just happy he knew a few letters of the alphabet. As far as I was concerned, he could call himself just about anything he wanted, if learning took place.

Another typical characteristic of autism is lack of facial expression, particularly smiling. There is not always a lack of a smile, of course, but sometimes the smile may come either at inappropriate times or for no apparent reason. Smiling for Daniel, once he started, was never a problem. He was a very photogenic child—if he was prepared or if it was his idea to have his picture taken. Everyone always complimented him on his sweet smile. To this day, that is one of the characteristics that people comment on the most—"Daniel always seems happy" or "I never see Daniel without a smile." Some people may think that it's odd that Daniel always has a smile, but I truly believe that he does feel happy most of the time. He does get upset and frustrated, but usually those feelings are short-lived. He loves to laugh, especially at my "Lisa jokes," as we call them. "Lisa jokes" are just really corny jokes that make me laugh even if no one else laughs. I'm a sucker for corny, and Daniel loves that.

It is very unusual to have a child on the autism spectrum who is not prone to meltdowns. Just about all children act out with a meltdown at one time or another, but with autistic kids, such behavior is more prominent and usually more frequent. I've witnessed children in the middle of a meltdown, and it can be very frightening. I'm sure it's frightening to the child as well. It's a loss of control with no solution, in many cases. Sometimes, children must be medicated in order to better control their spirals into the abyss of the meltdown. I do not know why Daniel never exhibited this common behavior. I'm thankful but baffled at the same time. Other than his screaming in the car for the first two years of his life, there were no other instances of temper tantrums or uncontrolled behavior.

An example of Daniel's compliant nature was evidenced one night about a week before our oldest son, Justin was about to get married. It was just Ron, Justin, Daniel and Allie Beth and I reminiscing about things in their childhood that they thought were funny or at least memorable. One of the questions Ron asked was "What was your favorite meal mom cooked?" Justin said "Chicken spaghetti." Daniel said, "Well, it wasn't the blue chicken." "Blue chicken?" we all asked at once. It took a while for me to remember, but I finally recalled one night when Daniel was about 10 years old. I wanted to cook something different and I thought, fun, for dinner. I was tired of the "same ol' same ol'". I remembered a dish my mom had fixed when I was child, 'Rice Krispie chicken." She would roll the chicken in Rice Krispie cereal and bake it. It was sort of the healthy alternative to fried chicken. Well that particular night I did not have Rice Krispies in the pantry but I did have Fruity Pebbles. Let's just say that when Fruity Pebbles melt, they turn a beautiful aqua blue. Well, maybe it's not so beautiful when it's on chicken. Daniel never said a word that night. I'm sure he just didn't eat very much. He waited 15 years to tell me about how he felt and even then it was because he was asked.

Daniel always has been a dreamer. He still comes up with the most amazing schemes and plans to either build something incredible or enhance something already existing. When he was about five years old, he wanted to build a fort in the backyard. We had already planned to buy a fort and swing set for the boys for Christmas. We went ahead and bought him a little hammer and nails and scraps of wood. It was all loaded in a toy dump truck under the tree on Christmas morning. When he saw the wood, hammer, and nails, he took them outside immediately to start building. Much to his dismay, he saw that a fort already existed—one that "Santa" had built during the night. I didn't know if it was a look of shock or disappointment on his face when he realized that he was not going to be able to build his own fort. He recovered pretty quickly, though, and enjoyed hammering his wood together. Whatever he created was awesome to him, and that's what mattered.

We could always hear Daniel coming because of the clanking from the toys stuffed in his pants.

Daniel accepted Jesus as Savior and was baptized.

Ice skating as well as Rollerblading were his favorite activities.

We learned to ski together.

Daniel settled on tennis as his sport.

One of our big goals was achieved!

Daniel's first time fly-fishing

Scary and exciting at the same time

Daniel had set a goal to have his driver's license by age twenty-five. He did it three days before his twenty-sixth birthday.

Daniel and Aubri—true friends

CHAPTER 8

Just to Reach Manhood

Listen! A sower went out to sow. And as he sowed, some seed fell along the path, and the birds came and devoured it. Other seed fell on rocky ground where it did not have much soil. It sprang up at once because the soil was not deep. When the sun came up it was scorched, and because it did not have sufficient root, it withered. Other seed fell among the thorns, and they grew up and choked it, and it did not produce grain. But other seed fell on good soil and produced grain, sprouting and growing; some yielded thirty times as much, some sixty, and some a hundred times (MARK 4:4-8).

Every parent dreams that his or her child will grow up to change the world—or at least a little part of it. No one says, "I hope my child just grows up and sits on the couch all day watching TV or playing video games." No one says, "If my child can just make C's and D's in school, that'll be great with me," or "I hope my son sits on the bench for whatever sport he chooses." We all want our children to be the best part of us and the best of who God created them to be, but sometimes, we just want them to be *the best*. We all want our child to be a star in one way or another—no one really wants his or her child to be average. This may be the reason behind the soccer mom or the football dad who screams at the child for making a bad play or at the coach for cutting the child from the team. When you know, however, that your child will never be the star, you realize how unimportant those achievements are.

As I've mentioned, Daniel's evaluations between the ages of five and seven were not encouraging. When the neurologists told us not to expect him to do the things that most children do, like ride a bike, Rollerblade, or play a team sport, I accepted that Daniel would never be the star of anything—but I would not accept his not being able to do whatever he wanted, at least on some level. He learned to ride a bike, Rollerblade, and was on a Rollerblade hockey team because I didn't want him to settle for nothing, not because I wanted him to be a star. We were shooting for average. I felt that would be a great accomplishment. And it was.

Daniel had always been somewhat accident-prone. With Justin, we were in the emergency room two or three times in eighteen years, with relatively minor injuries—a sprained ankle and of course, his seizures. Justin never had broken a bone or required stitches.

Daniel, on the other hand, had had seven stitches in the top of his head at age four from running into a door. He cut his knee on a bicycle fender, and that required stitches. He cut the back of his leg on a piece of broken glass in the trash bag while taking the trash out. The worst accident was at age thirteen, when he was jumping on a trampoline with his friend Heather. Although it's considered unsafe to jump on a trampoline with two people, most kids think it's fun to jump together and cause the trampoline mat to spring the other person up. We learned, however, that the force of the spring can break a bone.

When Daniel landed seat first, with his hands beside him on the trampoline mat, the force from the mat snapped his arm in half below the elbow. It was a compound fracture, although the bone did not quite break the skin. Thankfully, Ron was there and happened to be watching the kids when it happened. Daniel's high pain tolerance, while usually remarkable, had met its match—the bottom half of his arm looked like it had grown another elbow. It didn't take long for Daniel's pain—and our panic—to set in. I was inside the house, visiting with Heather's mom, when Ron yelled for me to come out. I climbed on the trampoline and held Daniel's arm together while helping him slide off into Ron's arms. We rushed to the hospital and waited for what seemed like hours for someone to take an X-ray. Obviously, his arm was broken. The doctor wrapped Daniel's arm in a temporary cast and told us we'd have to wait forty-eight hours for surgery. Daniel handled his pain incredibly well. We didn't get much sleep over the next two days, but we survived. The break in Daniel's arm required pins and a plate and left two significant scars on his arm—battle scars, we call them. Our new rule: no more trampolines! We managed to make the next five years relatively accident-free.

Because Daniel's pain tolerance is very high, we know that if he makes a noise that sounds like someone in pain, it must be really bad. This was the case the day I heard a thud on the stairs and then a moaning like an injured animal. Daniel had slipped on the stairs, bending his foot backward and causing a severe sprain in his ankle, which swelled immediately to twice its size. This happened just days before we were to take our family on a trip to Disney World.

Daniel's coordination struggles and the fact that he was having seizures, made walking with crutches, at best, a challenge. On the day I was trying to get Daniel to the orthopedic doctor, we tried every way we knew to get the crutches to work. I tried letting him hold on to me around my shoulder, while he used one crutch in his left hand. As we walked toward the door, the crutch slipped, and down we both went. We attempted to stand up, but I was not strong enough to lift Daniel, and he was not able to put any pressure on his right leg to help himself up. It was Friday, and Ron was out of town, so it was just my mother-in-law and me. We were of little help. I called two of my neighbors, hoping that one of their husbands might be home. No luck. Then I remembered that my friend and neighbor Tammy's husband was a professional football coach who had every other Friday off. I prayed that this was one of those Fridays.

When I called Tammy, I must have sounded panicked as I explained what had happened. No sooner had I hung up the phone than her husband, Jim, was knocking at my door. When he saw Daniel sitting on the floor, he tried to help him to his feet, but I explained that the crutches were not much help. Jim said, "Is it okay if I just pick him up?" Of course I said yes. Jim bent down and, in one scoop, had Daniel in his arms, as easily as if he were a two-year-old. He carried him to the car for me and even offered to go with us to the doctor to help us get out of the car and into the doctor's office. I knew that we could get a wheelchair once we arrived, so I declined his incredibly generous offer. I was so thankful for God's provision in that instance, to provide such assistance to us in our time of need. And we did make it to Disney World the following week—Daniel used a walking boot.

As I mentioned, once Daniel graduated from high school, we were in a dilemma of "what now?" After homeschooling and then finding a school, homeschooling and then finding another school, homeschooling and then finally finding a Christian school that would teach someone with Daniel's developmental difficulties, I was ready to say, "Enough!" We were not going to attempt traditional educational pathways again. We had made it through the worst part—high school. I couldn't fathom trying to navigate college entrance exams much less college itself. For the first time in our journey with Daniel, I felt we had come to the end of what could be considered "normal" for most children. I felt there was no way that Daniel could attend a traditional four-year college, live on campus, and expect any kind of typical college life. I wasn't even sure that he could navigate community college while living at home. Nor was it likely that he would be hired at a job that was anything more than sweeping or bagging groceries—not that there's anything wrong with those jobs. We are grateful for the retailers who hire special-needs adults in those positions. We just felt that if Daniel could do more, then we should give him that chance.

To add to our struggle, Daniel's seizures still were not under control. However through traditional medicines and some nontraditional approaches to medicine, Daniel's seizures stopped in early September 2004. We were cautiously optimistic, but this was a huge relief and blessing to us. After struggling through two years of high school with seizures every day, we were ecstatic that we might have a somewhat normal life for a while. We really didn't know how to define normal, but we were willing to see if we could find it.

From an early age, Daniel loved anything associated with the United Parcel Service, Federal Express, and the US Postal Service. He loved to point out the trucks to us and try to look inside the back of them. He often described how the boxes were stacked and how they could be stacked better. He would try to come up with elaborate conveyor systems to make it easier for the deliverymen to load and unload. Because of this interest, we thought he would enjoy working in a business that used those three shipping avenues. We explored the franchises that had popped up in recent years, such as Mail Boxes Etc. After looking at the franchise fees and other costs associated with opening a franchise, we decided to go on our own. We opened Liberty Postal Express as a small neighborhood shipping business in October 2004. This would be our first family retail business venture.

In the beginning, the entire family, including Grandma Dot, Justin, Daniel, my cousin Richard, and I, worked there together. Daniel learned the basics of the operation very quickly. Just like with the Ninja Turtles, this was something he was interested in, so he wanted to learn it. Don't misunderstand—I'm not saying that all of Daniel's learning challenges were because he just didn't want to learn, but when he found something he could latch onto, he did. There is no explanation for it; it just is.

We had the postal business for five years. By the end of the fourth year, instead of family members, we had our assistant, Dede, and Daniel working full time. Daniel was able to manage the business alone three days a week for most or sometimes all of the day. He knew that if he ran into a problem, he could call one of us, and we'd talk him through it. In addition, because we lived about a block away from the postal center, we could be down there in a flash, if necessary. Usually the problems were customer-related. If someone came in upset, even if it had nothing to do with shipping a package, Daniel picked up on it and felt that he was to blame. Those were the tough times, talking him through the scenario. "How did she come in?" we would ask. "Well, she was on her cell phone, and she was talking really loudly," he might say. "Okay," we'd respond, "then she wasn't mad at you. She was mad at the person on the phone." Once the scene was played back in his head through verbal coaching, he usually could see that he was not the cause of the customer's behavior.

Other times, however, he *was* the cause. People can be very impatient. Daniel was not the quickest person on a keyboard. Those pesky fine-motor skills and slight dyslexic tendencies still plagued him, so sometimes typing in the packaging information took a while. If the person wasn't in a hurry, it was fine, but if someone appeared agitated or irritated, it made matters worse. Sometimes, Daniel would just tell customers to leave their shipping information, and he would send the package. This was fine, as long as he also remembered to get their payment information, which wasn't always the case.

Before our five-year lease was up at the postal center, we knew we were going to have to decide what to do next. It had been a great relief to have a place for Daniel to have a meaningful occupation that was close to home and, for the most part, was a safe environment, but we were not making money at the postal center. It was never our intention to get rich, not by any stretch of the imagination, but we would have preferred to be out of the red most months. We tried to look at our cost of operation as college tuition. If Daniel had chosen to go to college, we would be paying about the same amount in tuition fees, so that was our justification for putting money into the business each month. But it had been five years. Even if Daniel had gone to college, this probably would have been his last year. In addition, we knew that Daniel needed a new challenge. We wanted more than anything to see how independent he could become. We set out to see what was available to help us transition him from total dependence to independence. Was there such a thing?

I began searching the Internet for some type of program that would bridge the gap between Daniel living at home and living either independently or going to college. There were several places in the United States, but none was in Texas. We visited two places that seemed to have the program and qualities for which we were looking. The first place, in Phoenix, Arizona, had a great plan and had been around for about twenty-five years. Certainly longevity was a positive point. Our family had vacationed in Phoenix quite a bit over the years, so Daniel was excited by the possibility of living there. The second facility was in Melbourne, Florida. We liked this location, because it was about an hour from Orlando, where Justin and his new wife, Amy, were living. Having a family member somewhat close by gave us a little better sense of security. We weren't as thrilled with Melbourne's program or living environment, but it was definitely in the running.

After discussing our options and talking to Daniel, we had decided to go with the Phoenix location. My mind could not fathom sending my son, who had never even been away to camp without me, over one thousand miles away where he didn't know anyone, but I was willing to try it, if it meant that Daniel would have a chance at independence.

The day we were going to call the Phoenix location to enroll Daniel, Ron had a chance meeting with someone at work who suggested using an educational consultant. I had never heard this term. You'd think one of the many therapists or doctors we consulted would have suggested getting in touch with an educational consultant, but no one did. I decided to try one more time to find something in Texas before we committed to Phoenix. I jumped online and searched "educational consultants, Dallas,

Texas." Pages and pages of consultants came up. I wanted to scream at each of them, "Where have you been for the last twenty years?" Instead, I clicked on some of the names, one of which linked to a list of programs for post-high school students with learning disabilities. I read the list carefully, and lo and behold, there was a program in Austin, Texas. I couldn't believe it! The College Living Experience (CLE) had several locations around the country, and their newest location was in Austin. I immediately called them and set up an interview.

Because Daniel has a special interest in politics, he was excited to learn about the possibility of moving to Austin, the state capital. He was a regular letter writer to our state representatives and governor. We were excited that Austin was only a three-hour drive from us instead of a three-hour plane ride.

Our interview with CLE went well. Daniel seemed excited about living and working with this group of people. They would help him become acclimated to college life, as well as teach living skills like cooking, cleaning, shopping, and budgeting. He was twenty-four years old and needed to feel that he was independent, even if it meant he was under the supervision of someone else.

We met with the staff of CLE in July and by the middle of August, we had Daniel's things loaded in a U-Haul trailer, headed to Austin. It was surreal, watching Ron and Daniel pull out of our driveway. I followed the next day to help Daniel set up his apartment. The apartments were across the street from the offices of CLE and down the street from Austin Community College. It was a regular apartment, not set apart or sectioned off from other residents. It was extremely scary for us as parents—overly protective parents, probably—and we wondered if we had taught Daniel enough about being leery of people who might try to take advantage of him. Had we told him enough times to keep his door locked and not open it without looking through the peephole? I wasn't as worried about his living skills, because that's what CLE would be there for. It was his "street" skills that worried me.

After we said good-bye to Daniel and were about to pull out of the parking lot, grief, joy, fear, and relief, all at the same time, overcame Ron—the reality of the moment was overwhelming. I was barely holding it together myself, but I had resolved that we had to do this. Even though Ron had, in his mind resolved as well, it was just the moment of reality that overtook his emotions. I had not seen him cry that way since my mother died 25 years earlier. Just an aside: Girls, when you find a man who cries when his heart is touched, you've found a man!

Daniel loved many things about the program at CLE. Mainly, he liked being around people his own age with similar abilities. There were scary moments for us, however, like when Ron happened to call one night, just as Daniel was writing a check to a magazine salesman who had come to his door. Daniel had opened the door without looking through the peephole, because he was expecting his friend Matthew. A situation like this was exactly what we feared. Ron was able to talk to the salesman over the phone as he stood in Daniel's apartment and told him that Daniel was not allowed to purchase anything. The salesman left and never came back. Crisis averted.

The program at CLE was meant to be a two-year program. While Daniel learned many things, for which we were grateful to CLE, we felt that after one year, he had received the benefits we intended for him. We had seen how he had matured and how his confidence level had soared. Daniel already had told us, shortly after moving to Austin, that when he moved back to Dallas, he would not be moving back to our home. He wanted his own place. We agreed with his decision.

Before Daniel moved back to Dallas, Ron and I searched for a suitable location for him to live and decided to purchase a condo in a gated townhome community. It was in a great location, with lots of retail businesses within walking distance—an advantage, as he had not gotten his driver's license yet. Daniel was very excited about his new home and the fact that he also would be able to work at Ron's office in Dallas, with about thirty of the greatest people with whom he could possibly work. We knew that Daniel would always need a safety net, as Ron called it, and that we, as a family, would be the main strings of that net. We have a group of people—family, a therapist, and friends—who help with things such as money management, learning to drive, navigating dating, and home maintenance, as well as answering questions— some as simple as "If this meat has been in the refrigerator for two weeks, do you think it's still good?"; some more complicated, like, "If God wants men and women to fall in love and get married, why does he make us so different?" (We're still working on an answer to that one!) With each lesson learned, we find something else that still needs to be addressed or at least needs a reminder. But such is life.

With the help of Jolene, Daniel's counselor at CLE, Daniel was able to pass the written portion of the driver's license test. We had found a program through St. David's Hospital in Austin that would teach driving skills to persons with disabilities. When Daniel called to tell us that he had just driven on the highway with his instructor, my mind tried to grasp it but couldn't. This young man, whom doctors told me would never ride a bicycle, was driving a vehicle on a major highway in Austin, Texas! I wanted to send every doctor, teacher, and other professional a video of Daniel driving, along with a recording of Toby Keith's "How Do You Like Me Now."

When Daniel moved back to Dallas the following August 2010, we had a friend who was willing to take on the task of teaching Daniel to drive. We were so grateful once again for God's provision through Neal Williams. When Neal got a job offer in another town before Daniel was ready to take the driving portion of his test, another brave young man, Aaron Lemmon, joined the driving team. Aaron was able to take over when Neal left. After a few more weeks of practice, Aaron thought Daniel was ready to take his behind-the-wheel portion of the test. Aaron took him to the Department of Motor Vehicles, but Daniel was unsuccessful. We decided Daniel should wait a while before trying again. About a month later, I took Daniel to the DMV. As he turned out of the parking lot with the person administering the test, Daniel hit the curb. I didn't know what that meant, but when Daniel came around immediately into the parking lot instead of finishing the circuit, I was pretty sure it meant he hadn't passed. The instructor said that hitting a curb was an "automatic fail." Daniel was disappointed. I told him we'd try again the next week.

Because we had instilled in Daniel to set goals and do his best to stick to them, he was determined to try again. His goal had been to get his driver's license by age twenty-five. Monday would be his twenty-sixth birthday. As he'd tried his second time on Thursday, he had only one more day to accomplish the goal—the DMV wouldn't be open on the weekend. Aaron said he'd gladly take Daniel early Friday morning to try again. I was so nervous. Although it scared me to think of Daniel with a driver's license, able to drive alone, I was just as afraid of his failing to achieve such a monumental goal.

The lines at the DMV can be very long, especially on Friday. The doors open at 8 a.m., and Daniel arrived a little after 7 a.m. It was extremely cold, but he stood in line with resolve. Shortly after 9:00, I received a text message from Aaron, along with a photo of Daniel standing in front of the DMV, holding his official Texas driver's license. The caption read "Texas's newest driver!" I didn't know whether to laugh or cry. I immediately sent the photo to Ron and then to all of the friends who had prayed for Daniel. It was a momentous occasion indeed!

CHAPTER 9

He's Always Been Mine

Certainly you made my mind and heart;
you wove me together in my mother's womb
(PSALM 139:13).

Our children are a gift from God. He gives them to us for an indefinite period for a purpose we may or may not see fulfilled. We are blessed to share their lives, but we may never know their ultimate role in this world. I think about families like the Bushes. President George H. W. Bush and his son President George W. Bush are certainly some of the rare and blessed father/son duos who were able to see at least a portion of what each other's purposes were on this earth. Of course, even they may not know their ultimate purpose—and if it was fulfilled—until they are before the Lord in heaven. Other families know their children or parents only for moments, days, or a few years and do not get to see any earthly fulfillment. But even those families,

I believe, would tell you that they would not trade the few precious moments with their child or parent for anything in the world.

You see, it's not about what we see as potential in a person or whether we get to see that potential fulfilled. It's about what God has put in a person and why he placed that person at the exact moment in time with the exact people He wanted to touch. I often had to concentrate on what God's purpose was for Daniel. Many times, I wanted to scream, "*Stop!* Just let me have some peace." I wanted to stop thinking about the "what ifs" for one day, one hour, one minute. I had to remind myself of the verse from Psalm 139:13-14. "For you created my inmost being; you knit me together in my mother's womb. I praise you because I am fearfully and wonderfully made; your works are wonderful, I know that full well." Or I'd remember Jeremiah 29:11. "For I know the plans I have for you, declares the Lord, plans to prosper you and not to harm you, plans to give you a hope and a future." It was not about my plan or Ron's plan; it was about God's plan for Daniel. Could I trust in an Almighty God? Could I trust the God who created heaven and earth to create in my son, in my heart, and in my family the beauty of His purpose?

As parents, we all worry about getting our children from birth to adulthood in one piece. More than that, we want our children to be successful and productive citizens. As a Christian, I added to my worry whether Daniel would understand God's love for him through his son, Jesus Christ. Justin and Allie Beth both came to understand at a fairly young age that they needed a Savior;

that they could never be good enough to get to heaven on their own. Of course, they didn't totally understand the concept of sin and forgiveness at the ages of five or six, but they knew enough to make that step of faith toward redemption. I wondered if Daniel would ever grasp that concept, and I wondered if it mattered. I know that there is grace for those who cannot understand such a spiritual concept. Was Daniel one of those to whom God would grant grace?

I have listened to a particular Christian radio station almost continually for over twenty years, KCBI, 90.9 on the FM dial in Dallas. It's mostly Christian talk shows and preaching, with a little music. It has grown and expanded over the years, and it is the greatest Christian radio station I know. One of the reasons I am so partial to KCBI is because of Daniel. As we'd make our trek to downtown Dallas to drop Justin at school and then go to Daniel's school, we'd listen to the radio. Each morning, a woman named Ethel Sexton had a short radio spot. She was known as the "Garage Sale Lady," because although she would do an uplifting short message during her time spot, on Fridays she would list all of the garage sales in the area. She would end each radio message by saying, "Make your own sunshine." Although I loved listening to her, I never thought about whether the kids were listening. On one particular day, we had just dropped off Justin off when Ethel said something about making sure that you know you're going to heaven. Daniel said, "Do I know if I'm going to heaven?" He had never asked anything about spiritual matters—I'd assumed he would not understand, even though he had been in Bible classes since he was a baby, and we read Bible stories at home. I said, "Well, Daniel, do you want to make sure you're going to heaven?" He nodded his head, so I said, "Then we will pray together that Jesus will come into your heart." He wanted me to stop right there in the carpool line, but I convinced him that we would have to move out of the way first. We drove the fifteen minutes to his school, and before he got out of the car, we prayed together that Jesus would come into his heart and be his Savior.

I believe that God answered my prayer for Daniel— that Daniel would be able to believe as anyone else would believe in God—by faith. The Bible says that we must believe as a little child. That's why the Gospel is so simple, so that "the least of these" can understand and accept such a vast concept as eternal life.

God, in his infinite wisdom, gave Daniel to us, not for our sake or for Daniel's but for God's ultimate purpose to be fulfilled. Will we ever know what that purpose is? Perhaps not. But I will never forget to thank God for allowing this speck of time to be part of His divine plan for eternity.

CHAPTER 10

I Would Have Said Yes

When we suffer for Jesus, it works out for your healing and salvation. If we are treated well, given a helping hand and encouraging word, that also works to your benefit, spurring you on, face forward, unflinching. Your hard times are also our hard times. When we see that you're just as willing to endure the hard times as to enjoy the good times, we know you're going to make it, no doubt about it (2 CORINTHIANS 1:6-7)[1]

We all dream, contemplate, plan, and maybe even scheme a little to create the ideal future for our children. But when a child is born with a disability, no matter the cause or the effect of the disability, we tend to lose a little bit of our dream for that child. Maybe a dad was a great sports hero in his high school or college.

---

[1] 2 Corinthians 1:6-7 (The Message).

It would be natural for him to want his son to follow in that path. But what if his son is born with cerebral palsy? Perhaps a mother is a great pianist and longs to teach her child the beauty of music and the thrill it has given her soul over the years. But what if her child is born deaf or with a physical deformity involving the hands? Those dreams come to a screeching halt and must be changed.

How do we, as parents, dream new dreams for our children when we have no idea what the future holds? First, we must realize that we never know the future anyway. It's easy to dream when we think of a perfect world, a world where all of our thoughts and abilities roll into one, and life is smooth and uncomplicated. Even when children do not have a disability, the son of the sports-star father might be gifted in music, and the piano virtuoso mother may have a daughter who prefers to organize and plan activities—we can't always plan our children's futures. When our dreams for our children get a reality check, we must remember the verse from Proverbs 22:6.

"Train up a child in the way he should go and when he is old he will not depart from it."

This verse has been interpreted many times to mean that if we train our children the way we want them to go—good, moral, athletic, musical, or artistic—then that's what they will follow for the rest of their lives—many parents look at this verse as a promise instead of a premise. Another interpretation, and I believe more appropriate, is that we must train our children in the way that they were *created* to go. If a child is naturally gifted in music, then training him or her to be a sports star will frustrate both the child and the parent. But if the child is given music lessons, who knows where he will end up by using that gift? There is nothing wrong with exposing children to different activities to broaden their scope of life, but to expect someone to become an athlete or a musician because we spend money, time, and effort on them will likely be an act of futility.

When it comes to dreaming new dreams for a child with a disability, sometimes we can do so easily and shift our focus, especially if there is an obvious physical handicap. But what about the child with a hidden disability like autism? How do we dream for a child's future when he or she cannot voice his or her opinion? How does the parent of a child who melts down at the sound of loud noises introduce him or her to the thrill of even watching a sporting event, much less playing on a team? Where do we find new dreams for the child who looks like any typical child on the outside but inside seems to have a world of his or her own?

The answer is, I believe, that we look to the Creator of that child. We can take comfort from Psalm 139:1-18.

> You have searched me, Lord, and you know me. You know when I sit and when I rise; you perceive my thoughts from afar. You discern my going out and my lying down; you are familiar with all my ways. Before a word is on my tongue you, Lord you know it completely. You hem me in behind and before, and you lay your hand upon me. Such knowledge is too wonderful for me too lofty for me to attain. Where can I go from your Spirit? Where can I flee from your presence?

If I go up to the heavens, you are there; if I make my bed in the depths, you are there. If I rise on the wings of the dawn, if I settle on the far side of the sea, even there your hand will guide me. Your right hand will hold me fast. If I say, "Surely the darkness will hide me and the light become night around me," even the darkness will not be dark to you. The night will shine like the day, for darkness is as light to you. For you created my inmost being. You knit me together in my mother's womb. I praise you because I am fearfully and wonderfully made. Your works are wonderful. I know that full well. My frame was not hidden from you when I was made in the secret place, when I was woven together in the depths of the earth. Your eyes saw my unformed body. All the days ordained for me were written in your book before one of them came to be. How precious to me are your thoughts, God! How vast is the sum of them! Were I to count them, they would outnumber the grains of sand—when I awake, I am still with you.[2]

God has never said, "Oops!" Your child and my child were given to us on purpose and with purpose. We may not understand what that purpose is, especially at first, but God does. I take comfort in knowing these two words: *but God*. They are written over and over in the Bible, and each time they prove that God knows, He sees, and He provides. When we cannot see His hand, we must trust His heart.

---

[2]   Psalm 139:1-18 (New International Version).

I do not pretend to be a perfect person, parent, or Christian. I am a mom. Ron is a dad. We are two people who have done the best we can with the gifts that God has given us—gifts that include our children. No parent is perfect. No parent is omniscient, but God is. In that fact, I found peace and the desire to keep going.

Daniel was 19 years old before a doctor used the word autism in a formal diagnosis. We wanted to have him tested one more time before we made a decision about what we should do post high school. While I had felt since Daniel was about 10 years old after reading a book by Temple Grandin, a leading author on the subject of autism and herself on the autism spectrum, that Daniel was autistic, I had never gotten a confirming diagnosis. Thankfully, having this diagnosis did not cause regret in the way we had structured Daniel's life. We probably would not have done anything differently. Once I saw the word 'autism' in a medical report, I was relieved, I had finally had validation.

As parents of a child with disabilities, we long for a friend for that child. We just want to know that our child is not alone or lonely. Before Daniel moved to Austin to enroll in the College Living Experience program, he had begun to form a friendship with a young man named Andrew in his Bible fellowship class at church. Andrew was a lay leader in the college department where Daniel attended on Sundays. He was the first person who seemed to take an interest in making sure Daniel was included in activities. He really was the first friend that I can recall Daniel having as an adult. As providence would have it, Andrew moved to Austin to attend the University of Texas shortly after Daniel moved to attend CLE. Andrew continued his friendship with Daniel by inviting him to UT football games or just to go grab a burger for dinner. Even after Daniel moved back to Dallas, Andrew stayed in touch and has continued to be a friend to Daniel.

God surely has shown us more than we could have asked or imagined through Daniel's life. One blessing that we didn't expect is Daniel's relationship with a precious young woman named Aubri McHugh. They met while at CLE but did not become close friends until after they both left the program. Aubri had finished the program four months after Daniel started and was living at home with her parents in Shreveport. Aubri's mother, Cathy, and I had spoken on the phone a few times before Daniel went to CLE and again while he was there. We had hoped that Daniel and Aubri would become friends, but it didn't appear that that was going to happen.

It wasn't until ten months later while Daniel was just getting settled into his new home in Dallas, that Cathy called me. I had spoken to Cathy only once since Aubri left the program so I was surprised to hear from her several months later. She and her husband, Bill were going to be in Dallas, and she asked if Ron and I would like to have lunch with them. We had never met in person, but we felt a definite connection. We agreed on a place and time for lunch.

When we started our conversation with Cathy, I knew exactly where she was headed: she was looking for a good friend for Aubri. Aubri, like Daniel, had had her share of hurtful relationships and bad influences. Cathy told us that Aubri remembered Daniel as being nice and that he hadn't participated in some of the more raucous activities that had gone after school hours at CLE.

While I had no idea how Daniel would react to this request for friendship with Aubri, I was more concerned about the logistics. Aubri was a full-time student at LSU in Shreveport, Louisiana, while Daniel lived and worked in Dallas. We decided we'd do what we had to do to make it work.

We were having a housewarming party for Daniel after he moved into his new condo. We asked Daniel if we could invite Aubri. He and Aubri had not been close friends at CLE, but he agreed that she could come. When Aubri walked in, she looked a lot different than the last time Daniel had seen her. At CLE, she had not put a lot of effort into her appearance. But the person who walked in to the party was an attractive young woman. Her hair was cut in a sassy bob. She was wearing makeup and a beautiful and classy black dress. Daniel lit up when he saw her. Once Aubri got there, it was as if no one else was at the party—and they have been practically inseparable ever since. I have a feeling that we may be planning a wedding in the future—talk about dreams coming true.

Daniel is now twenty-seven years old. He drives, lives on his own, and has a job and a girlfriend. I would say that from the outside, at least, that's a pretty normal life. We feel incredibly fortunate to have helped Daniel get to this level of independence. I realize that not every autistic person will achieve independence, but I encourage parents to be slow to say never. Even though in reality, there are things to which we *have* to say never, more times than not, "never" comes too quickly out of our mouths, and we don't realize that we're so close to accomplishing something huge. I've found, many times serendipitously, that by continuing to try something that was considered a never, we learned something else in addition or totally different from what we were attempting.

We have imagined all kinds of scenarios for Daniel since we realized he was going to struggle in many areas of learning and living. We tried to prepare ourselves, mentally and emotionally, for his being totally dependent on someone for the rest of his life—but we never gave in to that scenario. Our main goal for Daniel was always his success, in whatever form that happened to be. He has proven many experts—and us—wrong, over and over. Our greatest blessing has come through watching God work, not only in and through Daniel but through the people around him. It doesn't take long for people to love Daniel when they see his heart through his smile.

We are extremely blessed that Daniel was chosen to be ours although I'm glad God did not give me all of the details of what our lives would be like with Daniel. It would have been too much to comprehend all at once. Every life is made of joy and disappointment, and oh, the blessings we would have missed! The smiles we would not have witnessed. The funny, quirky jokes we never would have heard. The lessons we never would have learned from watching him work so hard on a task. Would we have known what the heart of God looks like without Daniel in our lives?

Sometimes I think God should have asked, "Daniel, do you accept this family as your family?" I hope that he would have said yes. I am so grateful that God allowed us to see our lives through someone who doesn't expect more than he gets; who accepts life but doesn't accept limitations. I pray that as you look at your circumstances, you begin to see God's hand, thank Him for giving you this "yes" opportunity, and then share your story with others. We were blessed insurmountably to have been chosen to say yes. How could we have said otherwise?

CHAPTER 11

Justin—The Brother's Perspective

The King will reply, "I tell you the truth, whatever you did for one of the least of these brothers of mine, you did for me" (MATTHEW 25:40).

When I first read Mom's e-mail, asking me to write what it was like growing up with a sibling who has a learning disability and autism spectrum disorder, I was a little confused. I didn't realize there is a term for Daniel's disability. I have always referred to Daniel as having learning differences. I'm not sure why I put it this way; probably more to make myself feel better about not having a sibling who is in any way disabled. Also, this response usually satisfied people's curiosity, so they would not ask any more questions. And for the most part, it inspired them to treat Daniel with courtesy and respect. The more I look back on growing up with Daniel, though, the more

I realize how saying he has learning differences is a gross oversimplification. I say this because Daniel's condition affects more than his capacity to learn in traditional ways. It does affect his mind and some basic cognitive function, but it also affects him in body and spirit.

Mentally, Daniel always has been sharper in the areas tested less often than those traditionally documented by the educational system. For example, I remember when I was eight or nine years old, I was riding in our car, along with some of my friends from school. One of my friends posed a classic biblical riddle to our van full of Baptist private-school-educated scholars: "How many animals did Moses put on the ark?" We all put on our thinking caps and went to work on the math, but before I could figure out two times anything, Daniel shouted from backseat, "Noah!"—meaning Noah had actually been the one to load the animals on the ark. We were all stunned, and having recently discovered my knack for memorizing all kinds of interesting biblical facts, I was humbled.

These moments of brilliance aside, Daniel definitely has struggled with the more academic elements of growing up. I remember getting upset with him when he would read something and guess the word, based on the first one or two letters. I wrote it off as laziness, having no idea of and even less compassion for the fact that his brain did not work in the same way as my own did. Like most people who carry a high opinion of themselves, I held Daniel to my standard. Looking back, I see how unfair that was, but back then, all I wanted was a brother who was just like me—able to think like me, joke like me, interact with others like me, and not beat me down with his "laziness."

This desire carried over into some of the recreational aspects of growing up. I remember when I was ten or eleven years old, I would think about that day when Daniel would be big enough and strong enough to compete with me at sports—the day when *I* could be the quarterback and him the receiver, when I could be the hitter instead of the pitcher, when we could actually play basketball together, but this day never arrived. Daniel has a great arm and turned out to be a pretty good all-time quarterback for me, but our competitions never reached the level I had hoped they would.

Daniel's lack of coordination also forced me to make sure he was somehow included in the games my friends and I played. He was always on my team. I did my best to ensure he was a part of the group, and I never let anyone criticize his ability. This was easy, because Daniel always played like he was the best. I see it now when he plays the drums. He believes he should be on the stage with John Mayer and plays with the same intentionality and ferocity as someone of a much higher ability. Daniel has rarely, if ever, suffered from self-doubt. He believes he can do anything, and if he finds out there is something he's not good at, he moves on and doesn't let it bother him. This tenacity and strength of spirit has been a gift from God.

I would like to focus on this strength of spirit. I truly believe that God bolstered Daniel's spirit with a supernatural awareness that allows him to see beyond his limitations and to wholeheartedly embrace what he can do—nothing gets him down for long. Daniel is the ultimate example of finding pleasure in the simplest of things. I have seen him most content when sweeping out the garage or washing off the back porch. Tasks that you and I may see as menial are tasks in which Daniel thrives. Not only does he enjoy them, but he completes them to perfection. I can remember myriad times when I've said, "Who cares if that gets done perfectly? Just get it done!" Daniel, though, isn't wired like me. He is wired to do a task fully, to completion, because he enjoys the journey to completion. He is not worried about what he has to do next. He is only focused on the task at hand. In that respect, I wish I could be more like him.

I'm smart, well coordinated, driven, and a dozen other characteristics that count for something in our society. Meekness, humility, and lowliness do not get you anything. Unfortunately, most people are living by the wrong economic standards. In God's economy, Daniel is the CEO, and I am the janitor. In God's economy, Daniel is the star, and I am in the stands. In God's economy, Daniel is the wise man, and I am the fool. I thank God for giving me an example of what it means to live a life of joy, peace, and humility.

Daniel's "disability" has taught me more about myself and helped me more with my shortcomings than I ever helped him with his. Though his condition may have limited him somewhat in mind and body, I truly believe God bolstered his spirit to a place where his limitations are almost irrelevant. If nothing else, Daniel has bolstered mine.

Blessed are the meek, for they will inherit the earth (MATTHEW 5:5).

CHAPTER 12

Allie Beth—The Sister's Perspective

As it is, there are many parts, but one body. The eye cannot say to the hand, "I don't need you!" And the head cannot say to the feet, "I don't need you!" On the contrary, those parts of the body that seem to be weaker are indispensable, and the parts that we think are less honorable we treat with special honor (1 CORINTHIANS 12:21-23).

Life with my brother Daniel has been difficult for me. Acting as the younger "older" sister is not an easy task. Daniel has been placed under the large umbrella of autism with a more specific diagnosis of Pervasive Developmental Disorder—Not Otherwise Specified, or PDD-NOS. When I was younger, I didn't understand why I had to be held accountable for someone who, to me, could take care of himself. I didn't get why even though I was the baby of the family, I didn't get treated as such. I hated the responsibility of taking care of a brother who is seven years my senior. In a way, I resented him. I knew it wasn't Daniel's fault, but in my mind, I blamed him. I just wanted him to be better, to be normal, to be more like our older brother. All of this was going on in my ten-year-old mind, and it was difficult to manage.

Because of my bitterness, I became somewhat hardened toward my parents, who always seemed to take his side. I resented my friends who all had such seemingly normal and happy lifestyles. And as such a young child, I didn't know what to make of it. It didn't seem like God knew what He was doing, as everyone always told me. I figured He had made a mistake, so I prayed every night that Daniel would be changed; that he would be smart and be like everyone else's siblings. It never happened, of course, and I'm so glad it didn't.

Though still one of my biggest struggles, in the past five years I've come to realize that Daniel's disabilities aren't about me, my family, or even about him. It's not God's way of punishing us, as I thought at one point. Daniel's disabilities glorify Christ in a way that I never can. Daniel truly has a childlike faith, and his naïveté and kindheartedness are characteristics of which I am so envious but can never attain. I've seen his kind heart. He doesn't let his disability control him, and my heart has been broken by that. I've witnessed firsthand a life lived under the constraints of mental disabilities, and the Lord has used these experiences to shape my heart into something that desires to serve others like my brother and to serve God through that. He has shown me what a true servant's heart really looks like, and I genuinely wouldn't have him any other way.

CHAPTER 13

Dad—Why Me, Lord?

*For if I do this voluntarily, I have a reward.
But if I do it unwillingly, I am entrusted
with a responsibility. What then is my
reward?* (1 CORINTHIANS 9:17-18)

"What have I ever done to deserve even one?"—isn't that how the old song goes? The singer questions how a sinner such as he ever could deserve the blessings God has given him. Likewise, when I think about Daniel, my question is also, "Why me, Lord?" With as much humility as I am capable of having, I wonder what I have ever done to deserve the blessing of Daniel Simmons as my son. It hasn't always been that way, however, and sometimes the question was turned from thankfulness to whining.

Well before Daniel was born, I had determined that it was important for me to achieve financial and career success, and the commitment to that goal was at the very top of my list. My thought process at the time (and to a certain extent today) was that striving for financial and business success was not in conflict with the eternally more important priorities of faith and family. Unfortunately, one of the things I have learned about my early adulthood priority management was that while I was physically around a reasonable amount of time, my mental attention usually had my career goals at the forefront. This was especially true during Lisa's pregnancy with Daniel. The main thing I remember about that time is that I was going to night school, working full time, and beginning to realize that since my last name was not Murphy, my career advancement at Murphy Oil had its limits. At the time, I was a benefit analyst in the human resources department and was at least seven levels away from the top echelon of Murphy. I had plenty of growth available to me at Murphy before hitting the glass ceiling associated with not being part of the family, but at age twenty-four, I was focusing on the limitations ahead of me and what I needed to do to avoid such limitations on my career path.

My solution was to move into an environment, both geographically and business-wise, where I was limited only by my talents and my efforts. During the summer and fall of 1984, while Lisa was busily caring for Justin and excitingly preparing for the birth of our second child, I was focused on finding a new job in a new city. The chaos that I was creating in our family never registered with me. I was convinced that my getting a better job in a place with more opportunities was my priority as a husband and father. Of course, I know now that a better balance between that priority and Lisa and Justin's needs would have served all of us better. The number one thing that concerned me as it related to the birth of our second baby was how this would affect my priorities. The possibility that this baby would not be just like Justin never once crossed my mind. Even when the ob-gyn told Lisa that she had excess fluid, which could be a sign of spinal bifida or some other mental or physical abnormality, I never thought through the consequences of having a child with unusual challenges.

I did get a new job in a new town, and two weeks after Daniel was born, I moved to Dallas, Texas. I am sure that even in the labor-and-delivery room, I struggled to stay focused on what was happening, while mentally planning the move and career change. As I enter a reflection period during my life's "halftime," I wonder if I would have realized the potential danger we were in that night if I had been more *present*. The doctor was late to the hospital, and during the ten minutes when the nurses told Lisa not to push, to wait for the doctor to arrive, was there oxygen deprivation that caused Daniel's developmental and learning challenges—and maybe even autism? If I had been on my game as a husband and father, could I have demanded another doctor or even that the nurses deliver the baby? Of course, we will never know. But I do know that God has given me the gift of making things happen and getting things done, and in this situation, I quite possibly failed both God and family. Given this possibility, I must ask, "Why me, Lord?"—but not in the way you might think.

It was reasonably early in Daniel's life that Lisa knew something was not right about Daniel's development. I became aware mainly because Lisa told me there were problems and explained to me what should be happening.

My thought was *Let's fix it.* Of course I couldn't, and even worse, I could not find anybody who could.

While I certainly experienced periods of frustration and anger at the situation and all associated with it, I had a specific turning point that moved me from pushing Daniel too hard to be normal and to overcome his challenges through sheer determination, to my realizing my role as protector, advocate, and most of all, friend to my son.

This specific turning point occurred when someone from the administration of the Christian school where Daniel had entered kindergarten—and where he was excited to attend with Justin—let us know that Daniel did not have the "gray matter" necessary to attend that school. I still can't think about that meeting without tearing up. It remains the most hurtful day of my life. The school that was dedicated to glorifying God could not adjust their teaching so that someone like Daniel could learn. Of course, we felt Daniel was smart enough, but he did not fit their learning profile. As you've read in Lisa's story, some of the best Christian schools in Dallas also turned us away. We quickly learned that when a school says it wants to educate children for the glory of God, that means children who fit the school's profile.

It was that fateful day when I turned from being the "pusher" to being the "puller" for Daniel. Since then, I have been his advocate and his buddy. It also was then that I turned from piteously asking "Why me, Lord?" to asking the same question as a thankful blessing for allowing me to be Daniel's dad. Here are some examples of my journey with Daniel:

Daniel's memory is prolific. From the time he was very small, if he put something somewhere or watched us put something somewhere, he always remembered where it was. He has found my keys and related stuff countless times. Anytime any of us loses something, we all just say, ask Daniel.

I traveled quite a bit when Justin and Daniel were growing up, and one time when Daniel was four or five, he asked where I was going. I told him I was going to Miami, which he heard phonetically as "my Ami." His response was, "I want to go to your Ami." What a moment of gentle, honest love from a son to his dad.

Daniel had motor-skill development delays, but he always, *always* persevered—from learning to ride a bike, to Rollerblading, to snow skiing, to playing tennis, to learning to drive a car. It may take him a little longer, but when he puts his mind to something, he always accomplishes it.

Here's a great story to demonstrate Daniel's tenacity: Lisa and I are goal-setters, and we have encouraged our kids to do the same. Daniel is a great goal-setter, and while sometimes his goals stretch the band of reality, he nonetheless works toward achieving his annual goals. A few years ago, I started taking my boys duck hunting, because we all liked the outdoors, and I thought it was something we could do together for a long time. Because of his motor-skill challenges, however, it is difficult for Daniel to load his shotgun by himself. Getting the shells in the chamber requires a good bit of hand and finger strength, and this is difficult for him. Two years ago, I learned that one of his goals was to be able to load his own gun—this made me weep. What an honest, simple goal—one that most would consider just something to "do." But for Daniel, it was an important goal, and so it became one for me as well. We worked on it together until he needed me to help him less and less. When we went out this year—a year later than his original goal—he did it and has kept loading his own shotgun all season. Victory, baby! Victory!

Daniel loves to travel, and he travels with me on my business trips quite often. We have been to Bucharest, Romania; London, England; British Columbia, Canada; Rio de Janeiro, Brazil; Kauai, Hawaii; and about thirty of the contiguous states in the United States. Daniel's easygoing attitude about most things makes him an easy traveling partner. He's interested in everything historical and political, and so am I. We make a great team.

One speech I developed for groups of entrepreneurs is titled "Participant or Crusader." I also gave this same speech at Daniel's graduation ceremony. The central theme challenges people to not just be a participant in life but to be a crusader, to get things done, and to be at the front of the pack. I end this talk by asking, rather loudly and pointedly, "Do you want to be a participant, or do you want to join me and others in being a *crusader*?" The first time I gave this talk at a business conference, the very first person who came up to me backstage was Daniel, telling me he wanted to be a crusader.

These are just a few examples of our life's journey with Daniel. There are many more, all equally fulfilling stories that remind me to be thankful and ask what I have done to deserve the blessings of being Daniel's dad?

As I've said, I love being Daniel's dad, and if I had been asked if I wanted this role, knowing the many challenges we could face, of course I would have said yes.

CITATIONS